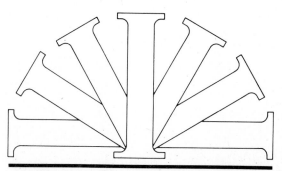

SHAPING COLLEGE WRITING

PARAGRAPH AND ESSAY

FOURTH EDITION

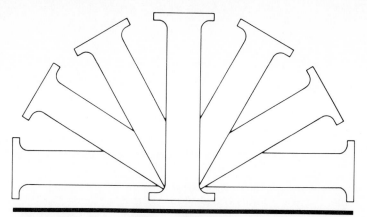

SHAPING COLLEGE WRITING

PARAGRAPH AND ESSAY

FOURTH EDITION

JOSEPH D. GALLO
HENRY W. RINK

FOOTHILL COLLEGE

HARCOURT BRACE JOVANOVICH, PUBLISHERS

San Diego   New York   Chicago   Austin
London   Sydney   Toronto

ISBN: 0-15-580863-X
Library of Congress Catalog Card Number: 84-81510
Printed in the United States of America

COPYRIGHTS AND ACKNOWLEDGMENTS

The authors are grateful to the following publishers and copyright holders for permission to use material reprinted in this book:

ANN ELMO AGENCY   For "Rosalie," from *Journal of a War* by Donald Pearce. Reprinted by permission.

ENCYCLOPAEDIA BRITANNICA, INC.   For the Shirley Muldowney biography by Victor M. Cassidy. Reprinted with permission from the *1982 Britannica Book of the Year*, copyright 1982, Encyclopaedia Britannica, Inc., Chicago, Illinois.

HARCOURT BRACE JOVANOVICH, INC.   For the excerpt from "Reflections on Gandhi." Copyright 1949 by *Partisan Review;* renewed 1977 by Sonia Orwell. Reprinted from *Shooting an Elephant and Other Essays* by George Orwell by permission of Harcourt Brace Jovanovich, Inc.

HARPER & ROW   For excerpts from *The Wheels of Commerce: Civilization and Capitalism, 15th–18th Century*, Vol. II, by Fernand Braudel. Translation from the French, Sian Reynolds. English translation copyright © 1982 by William Collins Sons & Co Ltd and Harper & Row, Publishers, Inc. Reprinted by permission of Harper & Row, Publishers, Inc.

THE NEW YORK TIMES   For "Black Youth: Prose Instead of Pros" by Arthur Ashe, February 12, 1977; copyright © 1977 by The New York Times Company. For the excerpt from "The Great Bridge and the American Imagination" by David McCullough, March 27, 1983. Copyright © 1983 by The New York Times Company. Both reprinted by permission.

RANDOM HOUSE, INC./ALFRED A. KNOPF, INC.   For the excerpt from *Alistair Cooke's America* by Alistair Cooke. Copyright © 1973 by Alistair Cooke. Reprinted by permission of Alfred A. Knopf, Inc.

SIMON & SCHUSTER   For excerpts from *The Age of Faith* by Will Durant. Copyright © 1950 by Will Durant. Reprinted by permission of Simon & Schuster, a Division of Gulf & Western Corporation.

VIKING PENGUIN INC.   For excerpts from *Black Lamb and Grey Falcon* by Rebecca West. Copyright 1940, 1941 by Rebecca West. Copyright © renewed 1968 by Rebecca West. Reprinted by permission of Viking Penguin Inc.

Preface

As a beginning exercise in composition, paragraph writing recommends itself on several counts. The paragraph is the smallest prose unit that lends itself to close analysis of unity, coherence, and systematic arrangement of thought. If well constructed, it resembles the complete theme in its support of a central idea by means of specifics. Ideally, it is long enough to demand some continuity of thought, yet short enough for students to grasp as a whole. At its best, it represents an essay in miniature.

As such, the paragraph seems to us to be the best medium for introducing students to pattern, structure, and arrangement in prose writing without immediately overwhelming them with the complexities of the full-length essay. Beginning students are too often asked to learn as many as twenty new skills at once and, what is more, to perform them all competently. Of course, practicing paragraph writing does not guarantee success for all students in every writing skill, but it helps them to master the fundamentals of good writing. Teaching students to make the eventual transition from the paragraph to the essay seems to us more logical than starting with the whole and then, only as a kind of afterthought, considering its parts.

Once students have developed a firm sense of the structure that underlies a well-organized paragraph, they are ready, we believe, to make the transition to the multiparagraph paper. By this time they have acquired the confidence that comes from learning to impose order on their thoughts. They have discovered that their ideas can be arranged systematically, that there are means of imposing coherence on diverse materials. And as they find the paragraph increasingly confining, they may also discover that there

v

is more in the world to write about than they had imagined and that they can exert some measure of control over what they finally do choose to write about. Most important, they see that the difference between a well-structured paragraph and a unified essay is one of size rather than of kind.

The movement from the most basic unit of paragraph writing to the construction of the whole paragraph is reflected in the order of the chapters in *Shaping College Writing: Paragraph and Essay*. The first chapter stresses the topic sentence with its important controlling idea, which helps students to focus their thoughts and organize their writing around the main idea of the paragraph. Chapters 2 and 3 deal with unity and coherence. Chapter 4 discusses specific sources of support and stresses the students' obligation to check and document the material they use. Chapter 5 directs the students' attention to the organization of the whole paragraph and introduces the similarities between the paragraph and the essay. In Chapter 6, students see the contents of the one-paragraph paper expressed in I-beam diagrams that show the rhetorical relationships of its beginning, middle, and end.

Chapter 7 allows students and instructors to extend the principles of organization and form of a one-paragraph paper to a multiparagraph paper. What we stress, in the generalizations governing this extension, is that the relationships are the same and the difference is one of scale. A five-paragraph paper is used as the archetype of longer essays, and students are offered what we hope will be a guide in future writing: the *one-three-nine structure*.

Chapter 8 discusses six fundamental methods for the rhetorical development of paragraphs: classification, definition, comparison-contrast, comparison-contrast definition, process, and description. We offer model paragraphs—some by professional writers, others by students—to illustrate each type of development. The paragraphs are generally within the framework of the I-beam shape.

Since this book does not pretend to be a grammar or a reader or a manual on usage, we recommend the use of any supplementary textbooks that instructors believe are suitable for their courses. We feel our book is adaptable to any basic composition course that emphasizes the principles of structure and concrete support as a means of teaching students to write. To this end, exercises have been devised not to offer students instant formulas for writing, but to help them recognize structural elements that characterize well-written prose.

We extend our gratitude to all our colleagues who helped us, joked with us, and encouraged us. But perhaps our greatest debt is to our students at Foothill College, who, over the years, have helped us to discover the pedagogical techniques that work in teaching composition.

Joseph D. Gallo

Henry W. Rink

Contents

8 Methods of Paragraph Development 150

The Topic Sentence

CHAPTER

1

The dominating idea of any paragraph is contained in a key sentence known as the *topic sentence*. This topic sentence—most often found at the beginning of a paragraph—contains the essence of the subject the paragraph deals with. The topic sentence is, of course, the most important sentence in the paragraph, and it takes the form of a *generalization*, which is supported or proved by specific facts in the remaining sentences of that paragraph. It may be helpful to examine the difference between a generalization and a specific statement:

A	**B**
Generalization	*Specific Statement*
Peter the Great of Russia was a physically awesome man.	According to Robert K. Massie, Peter stood 6 feet 7 inches and once knocked his erring prime minister, Menshikov, senseless with a single blow of his fist.
Oil spills are a tremendous threat to marine wildlife.	Small crustaceans forced by the spill to the surface are attacked by gulls, who become coated with oil and are unable to fly to shore.
For Napoleon, the Russian campaign was a disaster.	Of the 600,000 men of the *Grande Armee de la Russie* who entered Russia in June 1812, only 30,000 recrossed the Neman River back into Poland in December.

It is important to recognize immediately the difference between the generalization and the specific statement. Note that in column A the sentences are broader and less concrete. They resemble the large judgments we sometimes make about matters that concern us: "Medicare's a big bureaucratic mess"; or "Police programs are all the same on TV"; or even an old cliché like "Never judge a book by its cover." (Napoleon might have thought more about this last one before invading a sleepy-looking giant like Russia.) Notice another characteristic of the statements in column A: they are *judgments*. Almost all generalizations make a judgment or express an opinion.

The statements in column B, on the other hand, are not judgmental. Instead, they focus on specific objects or events. Each could be used to support its companion sentence in column A. The specific statements are more concrete—that is, they make reference to individuals (Menshikov), places (Russia, Poland, Neman River), dimensions (6 feet 7 inches), amounts (600,000/30,000), authors (Robert K. Massie), titles *Grande Armee de la Russie)*, and dates (June/December 1812).

From now on, generalizations (column A) will be used mostly as topic sentences. To support or develop these generalizations, specific statements (column B) are required. Specifics are the substance of writing; a generalization cannot be supported by other generalizations. You would look silly trying to convince thoughtful people that you knew what you were talking about if all you could offer them as support were vague generalities. For proof of this statement let's look at a paragraph that begins with a perfectly acceptable topic sentence about Tzar Peter the Great but which is followed only by generalities:

> Peter the Great of Russia was determined to change his country in positive ways. He was a man of great size and ambition, so nothing about the Russian government of his time pleased him very much. He was dissatisfied with just about everything he saw; he believed in self-improvement and national improvement. This sometimes made him hard to live with. He hated dishonesty, but what bothered him most was that people didn't want to do their fair share. All in all, Peter left the impression that he was a very dissatisfied monarch.

Notice that any one of the sentences in this paragraph could be substituted for the topic sentence. Each sentence is a generalization used in an attempt to support the main idea of the paragraph. As a result, one is left wondering what *specifically* bothered Tzar Peter so much. What do we really *know* about him after we finish reading the paragraph except that he was vaguely dissatisfied and that he *apparently* did something about it? (We never do learn what that something was.)

The writer might have named one matter Peter was unhappy with: say, the pitiful economic condition of the *serf* who worked the land. The writer might have told us of a single act of national improvement Peter devised: for example, his establishment of a central council to run the country while he was away fighting. Topic sentences like the one above cause the reader to ask, "In what positive ways did Peter alter his country?" It is the reader's right to have such questions answered by details/facts, and it is the writer's obligation to answer the question by providing details/facts, not a string of generalizations.

In college writing the approach taken in the sample paragraph above doesn't work because the writer does not produce facts that convincingly support the topic sentence. Good topic sentences imply a question that can be answered in the paragraph. The following are the kinds of questions a piece of writing might answer:

(a) in what ways?
(b) for what reasons?
(c) by what means?
(d) to what extent?
(e) under what conditions?
(f) with what results?

To be respected in a world where people think, you must be able to bring facts to the defense of your ideas. Don't be tempted to take the easy way out by writing a paragraph that is no more than a string of generalizations. Such writing raises more questions than it answers.

The Controlling Idea

Most workable topic sentences have three distinct parts: subject, verb, and controlling idea. The *subject* is what the sentence is all about; it indicates the general area to be dealt with. The *verb* makes a statement about the subject. The *controlling idea* usually follows these main parts and describes or makes a judgment about the subject, as in the following example:

subj   *verb*   *c.i.*

TS: In his novel *1984*, George Orwell proved to be more [accurately prophetic] than most people could have imagined.

In the example above you can easily see that the subject of the topic sentence (TS) is George Orwell. A unified paragraph on all a person's attributes (personal and professional) might run the length of a book. Therefore, the writer must select one aspect of Orwell's personality or accomplishments to be developed in the paragraph. The subject is then narrowed in the part of the sentence that describes or makes a judgment about the topic—namely, the controlling idea. The main function of the controlling idea (c.i.), then, is to focus, or narrow, the subject. Thus, the student using the above topic sentence would deal only with the events or political policies or scientific philosophies of the novel, written in 1949, that have become familiar aspects of our lives *today*. Under no circumstances should the writer begin talking about Orwell's personal life or his other novels, his popularity as a writer, his sensitivity, his poverty and poor health, or his personal eccentricities. Concentrating on the controlling idea *(accurately prophetic)* and applying it to the novel *(1984)* prevents much rambling.

True to its name, the controlling idea acts as a controller, or limiter, of what will be discussed in a paragraph. It may be viewed as a contract the writer makes with the reader—a promise to talk only about the portion of the subject expressed in the controlling idea. As soon as the supporting sentences stray from the controlling idea (violation of *unity*, Chapter 2), the writer breaks the contract made with the reader.

A controlling idea may take several forms. It may be a short phrase, as it is in the example about George Orwell. It may be simply a descriptive word, often an adjective, that refines or limits the subject. Consider the following:

   TS: According to Mother, Aunt Beatrice has become a [social outcast.]

In this topic sentence the controlling idea is made up of a noun and an adjective limiting or describing that noun. In a paragraph about Aunt Bea, the writer would develop whatever it was about her that made her so publicly unwanted. Perhaps the supporting details would answer two of the questions posed earlier: "In what ways?" and "For what reasons?"

Sometimes the controlling idea is a single descriptive word:

   TS: Most of her friends concede that Dr. Serena Dangerfield is [unpredictable.]

When a controlling idea is a descriptive word (often an adjective), as in the above sentence, you may find it helpful to define it, especially if it isn't a commonly used term. We know what *unpredictable* means, of course, but if the word you choose happens to be *munificent* or *sanguine* or *erudite*, you may need to look it up in a dictionary to be sure of its meaning. After all, it would be embarrassing to find, upon checking the dictionary, that a paragraph you labored to write has nothing to do with the actual meaning of the controlling idea.

Limiting the Controlling Idea

It is important that you recognize what your controlling idea is and that your controlling idea be limited and readily defined. You may also find it helpful to position the controlling idea near the end of the topic sentence so that it is the last thing the reader sees before getting to the supporting information. The following examples illustrate how topic sentences that attempt to cover too broad an area can be improved by limiting the controlling idea:

Rudimentary Topic Sentence	*Revision*
To me, Marie Curie was an interesting lady.	The physicist Marie Curie made some of this century's [most useful scientific discoveries.]

Interesting is the sort of adjective you might use to describe a modern painting that you don't understand but are too embarrassed to criticize; it's a vague word that gets you off the hook without committing yourself. *Useful scientific discoveries,* on the other hand, focuses on the accomplishments that made Dr. Curie "interesting"—that give us a more tangible basis on which to made a *judgment* about the subject. (She wasn't just vaguely "interesting"; she made certain specific scientific discoveries that led eventually to the medical practice of *radiology,* the treatment of diseases through the application of x-rays or rays from radioactive substances.)

Think how difficult it would be to illustrate the unrevised sentence in any concrete way—it's too vague and sweeping. But if you knew even a little about the scientific work of Dr. Curie and her husband Pierre, you could no doubt write a solid paragraph using the revised topic sentence. Let's try another example:

Rudimentary Topic Sentence	*Revision*
Grace Paley's "An Interest in Life" is a great short story.	In "An Interest in Life," Grace Paley deals with the fantasies and disillusionments of love.

Obviously, *fantasy* and *disillusionment* are more readily defined than *great,* a term too abstract to lend much focus to a subject. What makes "An Interest in Life" a *great* story is too complex to be adequately treated in a short paper, and what constitutes *greatness* is itself a philosophical issue that people have been debating for ages. The revision scales down the project and brings the writer closer to the story to begin the support. Remember, we have all probably engaged in romantic fantasizing and have all no doubt suffered disillusionment at one time or another. These are conditions that a student has a decent chance of describing in action; *greatness* is not.

It is in the controlling idea, then, that the writer settles on a direction and a focus. Up to the point where the controlling idea begins, a topic sentence could conceivably go in many directions. Think what might happen, for example, if the earlier writer chose to view Dr. Curie's accomplishments in a negative light.

The physicist Marie Curie made some of this century's [most *ominous* scientific discoveries.]

Such a ninety-degree alteration in its controlling idea, of course, would produce an entirely different kind of account—one that might focus on the role of Marie and Pierre Curie's discoveries in fueling the atom, and later the hydrogen, bombs.

Refining the Topic Sentence

As you have probably noticed in the examples above, the writer was able to improve each topic sentence—to make it more workable—by scaling down the controlling idea and positioning it near the end of the topic sentence. Now let's try to duplicate the actual process of creating and refining a topic sentence with its controlling idea.

Suppose you live near a road to an abandoned quarry where motorcyclists like to race and to climb slopes with their bikes. Every day you look at the riders roaring by, wearing leather jackets or ponchos, revving their motors, sometimes discarding empty beer cans and bottles along the roadside. Occasionally, you see the police arrive in response to a neighbor's call. The cyclists slowly disperse, but as soon as the policemen leave, the cyclists return to resume their sport. Eventually annoyed by the repeated disturbances, you might conclude that people who ride motorcycles are a pretty loud and low-life bunch. The process used in arriving at this conclusion is the same as the one by which topic sentences (and opinions and arguments) are made.

Now suppose you were to put that raw inference down in the form of a topic sentence:

Motorcyclists make pretty bad citizens.

Many writers might choose such a sentence, and, what is more, try to support it. But most first attempts can usually be improved. There is too much wrong with this sentence for it to be of value to you in writing a good paragraph. First, the adjective *bad* has countless applications, even in a small dictionary. Any term that can be so loosely applied to almost any undesirable situation is a poor prospect for a controlling idea. Second, people who create a public disturbance aren't necessarily "bad." Many law-abiding citizens sometimes disturb others with their activities—noisy parties, for instance. According to the topic sentence, however, you have committed yourself to proving that motorcyclists are bad citizens. Obviously, you aren't likely to prove such a generalization, certainly not in one paragraph.

What might be a more valid proposal to develop about motorcyclists? Suppose you try to restrict your proposition a little, to draw it into a more provable assertion. Perhaps you begin to think about the *reasons* for the riders' behavior, and you conclude that most of their actions are defensive in nature. So you try a new topic sentence:

Motorcyclists reveal their defensiveness by their public conduct.

This may be a little better, but it's still too big and a little vague as well. True, you could summarize the types of illegal conduct you have observed: the discarding of empty beer cans along the roadside, the removal of mufflers to give the bikes more hill-climbing power, the destruction of grass and ground cover by bike tires. You can also note the physical causes of these effects. But can you really perceive the *psychological* causes of the riders' conduct? You are only assuming that these acts reveal defensiveness; perhaps they simply indicate high spirits or disregard for public opinion or public peace. Then too, not *all* motorcyclists behave loudly and destructively. This topic sentence is too sweeping a generalization; you must try a different approach to the subject.

Perhaps you remember something your brother once mentioned about his own motorcycling activities. "With my machine under me," he said, "I feel I can do anything. My buddies feel the same way." On another occasion, when you asked him why he didn't just sell his chronically broken motorcycle, he said, "If I did that, there'd be nothing but me. And man, that's not enough!" From an article by Dr. Martin Milobar in *Psychology Today*, you jot down a quotation: "Victims of the motorcycle syndrome often experience a full-time preoccupation with the machine. Unlike the healthy cyclist, the compulsive rider feels diminished when he is even temporarily without his bike." When you question one of your brother's friends, he tells you, "The noise, you know, man? When you move in on a girl with your bike, it feels right." Now you begin to generate a more confident theory about *certain* motorcyclists:

> Compulsive motorcyclists reveal their lack of personal confidence in some publicly disturbing ways.

> *or* (to get closer to home)

> My brother Dominic's personal inadequacies come out in his feelings about his motorcycle.

You have evidence—quoted testimony from motorcyclists themselves and a statement by a psychiatrist—to substantiate your theory. No doubt you could find other material to support your topic sentence, which has now been narrowed down to a compact generalization—limited and definable. The process of creating your topic sentence took time. Along the way you had to reject certain notions and try to devise more sensible alternatives. But you will probably be happier with your third attempt than you would have been trying to support your first.

In Chapter 4 we will learn about the process of supporting the topic sentence with facts. Here we are concerned mostly with the controlling idea of the topic sentence and with whether that controlling idea can be supported within a single, unified paragraph. If you can't devise a topic sentence with a clearly defined controlling idea, chances are you won't be able to produce a successful paragraph—few paragraphs survive a poor topic sentence. Let's look at some workable topic sentences with their controlling ideas (descriptive parts) *italicized* and then defined:

1. The Papago Indian of the arid Southwest was a *tenacious* farmer.

   tenacious: "Characterized by keeping a firm, even stubborn, hold."

2. The ethnic makeup of Helsinki, capital of Finland, is perhaps the most *homogenous* among Europe's cities.

   homogenous: "Having the same composition, character, or structure throughout. Largely uniform."

3. Wisconsin University science professor Aldo Leopold always cautioned student writers against using *stilted* language.

   stilted: "Artificially formal or elevated in manner, pompous."

This brief list should give you an idea of the sort of topic sentence that has a chance of working in a well-controlled paragraph. Observe how each controlling idea points toward the facts that will be used to support it. In the first sentence, for instance, the reader might expect you to point out that the Papago built diked fields at the mouths of canyons, then relied on flash floods to irrigate corn, beans, and squash in a region that received only a few inches of annual rainfall. The fact that the flood occasionally washed crops away did not discourage the Papago. The writer of the second sentence will need to know—and point out—that Helsinki has no minority population to speak of, nor does it import workers from abroad to man its industries, as many other European industrial cities do. To illustrate the third sentence, the writer might provide an actual example of Professor Leopold's revision of a student's sentence. In a paper on the winter grazing habits of deer the student wrote, "The scope of this paper has been purposely limited to woody species common to the bear-oak type as it seemed desirable to lay particular emphasis upon the winter season when woody species were not only heavily utilized in general as browse but were even the sole food of deer following heavy snows." Leopold clarified the idea thus: "We studied woody plants because deer depend on them in winter, and during snow, may eat nothing else."

What we're saying is that the topic sentence points to the kind of facts that will be used in its own support. Notice also that the controlling idea is usually placed close to the end of the sentence. Strategically, the controlling idea might well be the last thing the reader sees before getting into the support itself.

One other characteristic of most good topic sentences should be noted: their *brevity*. It is a valuable rule of thumb for you to keep your topic sentences reasonably short. Of course, to write a long, sophisticated sentence isn't against any law. But the chances of your supporting some less important part of the sentence increase when the statement is wordy and involved. Consider the following perfectly workable topic sentence (which Professor Leopold would have red-penciled brutally).

> While it suffers from overcrowded and traffic-ridden cities, outmoded technology, and a high illiteracy rate, the Middle Eastern nation of Oman—once a center for the East African slave trade—is a staunch ally of the West.

The writer who devises such a sentence runs the risk of focusing on the fact that more of Oman's citizens need to learn to read or that Oman once conducted a profitable trade in slaves. Perhaps all these considerations have their place in a paragraph. But the important point is that crowded, backwards Oman is one of America and Europe's most loyal friends; that's the point that needs to be supported. That's also the point that could get lost in the sentence. If you can't resist the urge to create long topic sentences, you should at least remember to place the principal idea in the main or independent clause. (We will discuss the importance of main clauses in the next chapter.)

A more urgent warning should be delivered about topic sentences that are likely to be losers from the start. Avoid what is sometimes called the *dead-end* topic sentence, one that either lacks a controlling idea or fails to point in any direction:

1. T. A. Edison invented the incandescent bulb.
2. In a single rainfall season—June 1981–June 1982—255 inches of rain fell on Wilder Ridge, southern Humboldt County, California.
3. Wild seeds are carried from one place to another on the wind.
4. Polynesian people sailed to Hawaii from the Marquesas more than a thousand years ago.

None of these statements lends itself to unified paragraph structure. None points toward any concise group of facts that could support it. Each lacks a controlling idea and tends to be too factual (thus insufficiently judgmental) to act as a supportable proposition. Not one of them is the least bit arguable.

The *wild guess* is another kind of topic sentence that you should avoid. Note the following:

1. By the end of the century, the European Common Market will probably be rendered bankrupt, NATO ineffective, and the UN obsolete.
2. Our difficulties with Iran will end when the present Teheran government is supplanted by more moderate leadership in the decade of the eighties.

You must admit that it would be difficult to find facts to support these generalizations. No facts exist, of course, that will reveal precisely what will happen next year. Only an expert can make an educated guess about the future on the basis of present trends. Remember, you are a writer, not a fortuneteller.

Finally, it is a good policy to avoid posing a *question* as a topic sentence:

1. What are the cardinal rules one must follow to be successful in life?
2. How can one continue to maintain his or her optimism in a society dedicated mostly to the mindless pursuit of pleasure?

How indeed? Important as these questions may be, you could ramble on and on about them. Assert yourself! Know what you're writing about. Don't be tentative or questioning when you have facts to support an idea. Make the topic sentence a statement, an assertion—not a cry for help.

SUMMARY

1. The topic sentence contains the dominating idea that will be developed in the paragraph.
2. The topic sentence should be placed at the beginning of the paragraph because it is easier to form a paragraph from a key idea than to lead up to that idea.
3. The topic sentence is the writer's promise to the reader to deliver factual support.
4. The controlling data is the essential descriptive or judgmental or argumentative part of the topic sentence.
5. The controlling idea is the word or phrase that is limited and readily defined.
6. The controlling idea is best placed toward the end of the topic sentence.
7. Although the topic sentence may contain more than one clause, it is best to keep the sentence brief and to the point.
8. If you choose a complex topic sentence, the controlling idea should appear in the main clause. (Clauses will be discussed at greater length in the next chapter.)
9. Avoid the dead-end topic sentence, which lacks a controlling idea and points in no direction whatsoever.
10. Avoid the prediction (wild guess) and the question as topic sentences.

Writing a good topic sentence takes time and practice. You must often discard several prospective sentences before narrowing down the final product to a workable unit. But achieving a good topic sentence is essential and worth the effort involved. For though it wouldn't be true to say that a good topic sentence unconditionally guarantees a successful paragraph, without one you might just as well file your notebook and go to a movie.

EXERCISE 1   *In the blank at the left, write* **G** *if the sentence is a generalization and* **S** *if it is specific.*

_____ 1. During the Middle Ages, punishment for even minor crimes was often quick and inhumane.
_____ 2. *Blue Highways* is an American travelogue written by William Least Heat Moon.
_____ 3. Sharks, rays, and skates belong to a subclass of fishes called *elasmobranches.*
_____ 4. Spelunking, or exploring caves, is risky business.
_____ 5. The Mississippi is the mightiest of America's rivers.
_____ 6. The War of 1812 was fought at sea.
_____ 7. Mother Theresa won the Nobel Peace Prize in 1980.
_____ 8. Mother Theresa combines compassion with administrative toughness.
_____ 9. Many of the TV news programs one watches are mostly flash and fluff.
_____ 10. Mark Spitz won seven gold medals in the 1972 Olympics, more than anyone in history.
_____ 11. In journalism, what is important is not always sensational, and vice versa.
_____ 12. A loving family nurtures emotionally healthy children.
_____ 13. An affectionate family constitutes the soil in which a child blossoms.
_____ 14. The East Brother Light Station of San Francisco Bay was built in 1873–4.
_____ 15. San Francisco Bay can be a treacherous waterway.
_____ 16. The famous Radio City Rockettes—women who do a high-kicking dance onstage—have always numbered thirty-six.
_____ 17. Some dancing groups have become famous for their routines.

EXERCISE 2   *The aim of this exercise is to clarify the distinction between a generalization and a specific. For each of the following sentences, supply one or two facts that support the generalization. (Option: you may develop a paragraph from any one of the sentences.)*

Example: Attending college is expensive nowadays.

Fact: Tuition this semester is about $500, an increase of $125 over last year's.

Fact: I spent $150 on books for five classes and supplies.

1. Enrolling for classes in this college was relatively easy.

   Fact: _____

   Fact: _____

2. Enrolling for classes in this college/university presented some difficulties.

   Fact: _____

   Fact: _____

3. My counselor gave me some good advice when I signed up for classes.

   Fact: _____

   Fact: _____

4. This college/university provides supporting services for its students.

   Fact: _____

   Fact: _____

5. Like many beginning students I'm learning that I need to spend more time doing homework than I did in high school.

   Fact: _____

   Fact: _____

6. Anatomy and physiology (or _____) is the most challenging course I'm taking this term.

   Fact: _____

   Fact: _____

7. Health and fitness (or _____) is the least demanding course I'm taking this term.

   Fact: _____

   Fact: _____

8. The instructor of this class has certain mannerisms that attract the student's attention.

   Fact: _____

   Fact: _____

9. In guidance and orientation, I got some advice intended to help me study more effectively.

Fact: _____

Fact: _____

10. Detailed requirements for this class have been spelled out in the course description.

Fact: _____

Fact: _____

EXERCISE 3   *In each of the following topic sentences, underline the word or phrase that constitutes the controlling idea. Remember that the controlling idea is the focal element of the topic sentence that will be developed in the paragraph.*

1. For immigrants from Southeast Asia, gaining acceptance in American society can be a tough struggle.
2. The attitude towards feminism in the Arab nations is antagonistic and backwards.
3. Pineapple growing and harvesting is a labor-intensive industry.
4. The great white shark is considered to be by far the most aggressive and dangerous creature in the sea.
5. The island of Molokai in the Hawaiian chain is famous for its remoteness and solitude.
6. For farmers whose crops depend on irrigation, free-flowing rivers—rivers without dams—can be a very uncertain resource.
7. People suffering from AIDS (Acquired Immune Deficiency Syndrome) are considered by hospital staffs to be high-risk patients.
8. In *Challenger's* 1983 flight, Dr. Sally Ride proved that being a woman is no disadvantage in space.
9. John F. Kennedy's White House tapes reveal a man who was tense, incisive, and wry.
10. Dams have had far-reaching ecological effects upon the Colorado River.

EXERCISE 4   *Many of the following topic sentences are either dead-end or lacking in direction. Choose the one from each group that seems best suited for development in a paragraph. Look for the sentence that most effectively narrows down to a workable controlling idea. Underline that idea.*

1. a. Grey Whales are the most public and playful of whales.
   b. Each year, Greys make a 6,000 mile migration from Alaska.
   c. It takes three months to migrate to the breeding grounds in Baja California.

2. a. Like porpoises, whales can bounce sounds off objects while under-way.
   b. Whales have occupied this planet for 30 million years.
   c. Commercially, whales are the marine species most useful to man.

3. a. Between November and April, the Amazon River can rise as much as forty feet.
   b. Ecologically, the Amazon is one of the earth's most fertile sources of life.
   c. Two thousand species of fish are found in the Amazon.

4. a. In 1741, the Russian explorer Vitus Bering surveyed the straits be-tween Alaska and the Soviet Union.
   b. Bering died in these straits, and today they bear his name.
   c. Although small, the Bering is one of the world's most dangerous and unpredictable seas.

5. a. The main ingredient in natural gas is methane, a hydrocarbon.
   b. Natural gas is America's most plentiful and economical domestic fuel source.
   c. One-fourth of the energy America uses comes from natural gas.

6. a. Between 1927 and early 1932, Henry Ford produced nearly five million Model A Fords.
   b. The Model A was popular because of its dependability and stamina.
   c. It is estimated that there are still nearly a million Model A's on the road in America.

7. a. From 1933 to 1942, the Civilian Conservation Corps employed 2.5 million men.
   b. The press called the CCC "Roosevelt's tree army."
   c. During the Great Depression the work of the CCC was of great benefit to the nation's parks and forests.

8. a. In the spring, one can take a jet-boat cruise on the Klamath River, leaving Requa and traveling about thirty miles upstream to the Hoopa Indian Reservation.
   b. The Klamath is California's "river for all seasons."
   c. In the winter fishing is possible all along the upper Klamath.

9. a. Margaret Mead's *Coming of Age in Samoa* was a study of sexual practices among young Polynesians.
   b. When Mead was doing anthropological research in Samoa, she often worked ten or fifteen hours a day.

c. According to some anthropologists, Margaret Mead's Samoan theories show her excessive love of generalizations.

10. a. A polar bear can pull a seal up through a small hole in the ice so savagely that it crushes all its victim's bones.
    b. Polar bears are incredibly powerful creatures.
    c. A polar bear has been known to tear off a man's arm with one vicious swipe of its paw.

EXERCISE 5   *Devise a topic sentence to accommodate each set of facts listed below. Be sure that the controlling idea is the logical summation of the facts given and that it accounts for all the facts.*

discuss in class

Misconceptions about bats

1. a. Bats are not blind; they see reasonably well.
   b. Bats take excellent care of their fur, grooming themselves constantly.
   c. Bats do not get entangled in people's hair.
   d. Bats are seldom rabid; when they are, they are rarely aggressive.

   _____

The contributions of bats

2. a. Tropical bats may have been the earth's first fruit and flower pollinators.
   b. Bats consume enormous quantities of night-flying insects, including mosquitoes.
   c. Certain bats destroy and consume mice, helping to keep the mouse population under control.
   d. Like birds, bats disperse—through their wastes—the seeds of valuable plants over a wide area.

   _____

Environmental problems in Venice

3. a. In Venice, rising winter tides regularly flood the squares of the city five times more frequently now than they did in the past.
   b. Many of Venice's buildings are slowly sinking, or leaning.
   c. When waters recede, salt and moisture remain inside the walls causing mortar to decay.
   d. The sulphur fumes from nearby industry mix with air moisture to form sulphuric acid that eats away the stone of statues and marble monuments and even affects paintings.
   e. The filling in of mud flats has caused alterations in the tides that cleanse Venice's canals of sewage and waste.

   _____

4. a. Staphylococcus—an ancient disease—continues occasionally to threaten hospital patients despite modern antiseptic procedures.

b. In spite of purification techniques used to kill them, harmful organisms carried in drinking water still can and do end up in human blood.

c. A recent outbreak in Minnesota of salmonella, an intestinal disease, was traced ultimately to a herd of cows in South Dakota.

d. In 1980, an outbreak of toxic shock syndrome among women originated with a product that, for all intents and purposes, had been carefully produced under sanitary conditions.

e. In 1976, an innoculation campaign designed to safeguard Americans against swine flu caused a serious partial paralysis in about 100 people.

5. a. Russians—Slavic people who comprise just over half of the Soviet Union's population—live throughout that nation and hold many educated positions.

b. In southeastern Russia, Kazakh horsemen of Moslem religious heritage speak Turkic and still live in circular tents called *yurts.*

c. The Uzbek people of the Southeast, Islamic cotton growers, are the third-largest Soviet ethnic group—famous for their fabled cities of Tashkent and Samarkand.

d. Western Russia is home to the Ukrainians, the Soviet Union's second-largest ethnic group. Most of the Cossack horsemen were Ukrainian.

e. In the northeast, the Asiatic Chukchi are nomadic reindeer herdsmen who number only about 13,000 and resemble American Eskimos in dress and appearance.

f. Yakuts are northern Siberian people who for centuries survived on the milk of their horses and now grow a weather-resistant wheat important to the Soviet economy.

6. a. In the 1920s, the late Buckminster Fuller designed the so-called "Dymaxion House," a moveable, glass-walled structure that revolutionized architecture.

b. Fuller conceived the dymaxion three-wheeler, an automobile that even in the early thirties could go over 115 miles per hour.

c. Fuller's dymaxion map was the first flat-surfaced map to present landmasses that did not appear distorted.

d. After World War II, Fuller received a patent for his geodesic dome, a hemispheric structure that used less construction material and featured more living space than other buildings.

7. a. Three thousand years before Christ, the people of the Middle Eastern country called Sumer used a wheeled cart, the probable forerunner to all land vehicles.

   b. The Sumerians used metalworking techniques to produce bronze by adding 10 percent tin to 90 percent copper.

   c. The Sumerians developed the potter's wheel, still used to produce crockery today.

   d. Five thousand years ago, Sumerians cut wedge-shaped word pictures on clay tablets—a technique called "cuneiform." Sumerian script was not merely picture writing but a bonafide form of literacy.

---

8. a. During Holy Week, the Cora Indians of Mexico reenact the arrest, persecution, and crucifixion of Christ by choosing certain members of the tribe to play the role of *borrados*, the original Judeans who crucified Jesus.

   b. The *borrados* stain themselves with soot and mud, thus "erasing" their personalities and escaping responsibility for what they will do.

   c. The *borrados* run frenziedly through the village, carrying long poles as weapons in a reenactment of the mob that accosted Jesus. From time to time they abuse the townspeople, even hitting an onlooker occasionally with a pole.

   d. On Holy Thursday, a young boy assumes the role of Jesus and tries to escape on foot from the *borrados*, who pursue him through the village and out into the countryside. He must escape three times before he is captured and symbolically crucified the following day, Good Friday.

   e. On Saturday, the village governor "defeats" the *borrados* in battle, marking Jesus' resurrection. The *borrados* writhe on the ground in feigned agony as good triumphs over evil.

---

9. a. Park police at Staten Island's Gateway National Recreation Area have had to assist coastguardsmen in intercepting and confiscating narcotics bound for New York.

   b. In Texas, drug smugglers from Mexico have shot at rangers in Big Bend National Park.

   c. In California's Angeles National Forest, a popular vacation spot, motorists camping in remote areas have been robbed and even murdered.

   d. Tragedy has resulted from visitors' feeding of bears in Yellowstone, America's oldest national park.

e. Slides take vacationers' lives each winter in Montana's Glacier National Park.

10. a. Golog women of Tibet often braid their hair in 108 strands, a number that carries religious significance for local Buddhists.
   b. If a Golog rider likes someone, he will cut a lock of hair from his visitor's head, one from his own, and one from his horse. He will twine the three and tie them to a shrine pole.
   c. The Tibetan Buddhists spin colorful wheels on which certain prayers are inscribed. The spinning sends the prayers to heaven.
   d. Certain Tibetans worship Mount Anyemaquen, named for the mountain god Maquen Bomra.

EXERCISE 6   *Do exactly as you did in the preceding exercise.*

1. a. Shortly after Germany fell in 1945, former Gestapo colonel Rudolph Beulher was hired by U.S. Counter Intelligence to gather information on the Russians.
   b. Beulher, suspected of being responsible for the murder of over 5,000 Frenchmen, also worked for the British, who eventually got him a passport to Honduras.
   c. In Tegucigalpa, Beulher worked for the Honduran government as an agent to Mexico assigned to uncover industrial espionage.
   d. Beulher made two recent business trips to the U.S. under the name Dieter Meister; he discovered top-secret CIA plans to "stabilize" the political situation in Central America.
   e. Last month, Beulher—once nicknamed the "Rack of Rouen" for his torture practices—slipped unnoticed in and out of France where he stole plans for the French defense of Chad against the Libyans.

2. a. In August 1983, Hurricane Alicia "imploded" hundreds of windows in high-rise hotels, blowing them inwards and sending guests crouching for hours in hallways.
   b. Alicia picked up a car on a Galveston, Texas, overpass and deposited it relatively undamaged in a parking lot a block away.
   c. The hurricane imbedded straw and twigs into the surface of cement buildings.
   d. A missing horse that had been grazing in his owner's pasture turned up browsing peacefully on an island three miles out in the Gulf.

e. In Houston, Alicia tore open the 30-story high lobby-atrium of a luxury hotel and blew a twister of wind and water into it.

---

3. a. Bees collect pollen from the yellow flowers of the paloverde bush during the blooming season of late spring.
   b. Many small rodents, like the antelope ground squirrel, feed on the seeds of the paloverde.
   c. One of the few tall plants in the desert, the paloverde is used as a nesting site.
   d. Large animals, like the black-tailed jackrabbit, use fallen limbs at the base of the paloverde for shade and for concealment from predators.
   e. Mistletoe, which grows as a parasite on the paloverde, is a favorite food of the phainopepla and other birds.
   f. Bighorn sheep browse the tender stems and leaves of paloverde.

---

4. a. Silver, long considered one of the world's precious metals and a standard for currency, is used to plate the bearings of jet engines and diesel locomotives because it is a natural dry lubricant.
   b Because of its image-making power, silver grains are used in the process of color film development.
   c. Silver is used in the tiny oxide batteries that power hearing aids.
   d. Sixty metric tons of silver a year go into dental fillings for Americans alone.
   e. Silver conducts heat and electricity better than any other metal, including copper; 5/100 of an ounce of silver can be drawn into 400 feet of wire.

---

5. a. In 1982, a California truck driver attached a lawn chair to forty-two helium weather balloons and flew the contraption to 16,000 feet. He descended by gradually popping the balloons individually with an air gun.
   b. In 1970, Rick Sylvester, wearing a parachute, skied off Yosemite's El Capitan and floated safely to earth more than a mile below.
   c. Joe Tong, flying a 250 pound ultralight plane, went from California to New York in a record eighteen days. He is now talking of flying an ultralight to the North Pole.
   d. Photographer Peter Bird last year singlehandedly rowed an aluminum boat 9,560 miles in 296 days from San Francisco to Australia's Great Barrier Reef.

e. Grace McGuire, a New Jersey pilot, plans to fly a plane identical to the late Amelia Earhart's from New Guinea to mid-Pacific, using no more fuel than Earhart carried in 1936.

---

6. a. Cacti and other succulents are built to store whatever moisture they receive. Their cylindrical shape reduces evaporation.
   b. Since water readily evaporates from the surface of leaves, many desert plants have small leaves (burroweed), coated leaves (creosote bush), or no leaves at all (smoke tree).
   c. Some desert plants produce leaves only when there is moisture available (ocotillo). When the drought returns, they quickly shed the leaves. Should the drought continue, many species can lose their other branches as well, leaving only a few withered stems and their roots (bulbs) underground.
   d. Some plants may use a combination of all the above methods to live in the desert.

---

7. a. Eskimo hunters of the Bering Sea believe that the *inua* (spirit) of an animal enjoys being hunted with beautiful weapons, so they carve intricate harpoon-heads out of ivory.
   b. Northern hunters often carry lance points inside a box shaped like a baby seal riding on its mother's back. They believe the points become acclimated to being inside the seal and that the live seal will thus more readily "accept" the point.
   c. In their ivory carvings, Eskimos depict symbolic moments of the hunt, as in an enormous bird grasping a seal with its beak and claws. Such carvings are carried along on the hunt as good luck amulets.
   d. An iron thong used to drag a slain seal over the ice has a whalebone handle carved in the shape of a wolf's head. Eskimos believe that the implement will take on the predatory qualities of the wolf and thus become a more potent tool.
   e. An Eskimo ceremonial mask of a black bear is supposed to capture the bear's *inua* and transfer it to the mask wearer.

---

8. a. After Glen Edwards of the Pittsburgh Steelers knocked out Cincinnati quarterback Ken Anderson with his forearm, Edwards said, "I would have delivered the same blow if it had been my own mother." This comment gets laughs at banquets, where Edwards earns money as a speaker.

b. Says George Petoska, a coach in the National Football League, "Good holding is respected. The Raiders and Miami are two real good 'holding' teams. Everybody would like to do it as well as they do." "Such a comment," said one reporter, "makes cheating look like an art."

c. When Dallas Cowboys' Cliff Harris laughed at a mistake by Pittsburgh's Jack Lambert, Lambert flung Harris to the ground like a rag doll. The more he has done such things, the more Lambert has been asked to speak and to endorse products—a very profitable activity for athletes.

d. St. Louis guard Conrad Dobler has been called "the dirtiest player in football." He has been known to hold, bite, and punch during a game. Dobler says, "If those guys want to play dirty, then they're playing right into my hands, because I've played dirty a lot longer than they have." Dobler's salary is one of the highest of any lineman in the NFL.

---

9. a. Completed in 1883, the Brooklyn Bridge was the first suspension bridge to use steel cables in place of wrought iron, a feature used later on bridges like the nearby Manhattan Bridge.

b. The Brooklyn Bridge used a single span, just as the Golden Gate was later to use.

c. The 85-foot-wide deck of the bridge had tracks for a cable railway with carriageways running alongside; it was the first single-span bridge designed to carry both rail and vehicular traffic, a common practice today.

d. The footings to the towers of the Brooklyn Bridge required air-tight chambers—pumped full of compressed air—that were sunk into the riverbed and filled with concrete, a technique used on newer bridges that spanned large waterways, like the Oakland Bay Bridge.

---

10. a. During World War II, Geoffrey Pike proposed construction of a mammoth aircraft carrier out of ice strengthened by sawdust to operate in the North Atlantic, a proposal given serious consideration by Lord Mountbatten. Smaller boats made of ice had been used by Northern native hunters.

b. Pilings for supporting buildings in northern Alaska are set in ice holes, then filled with sand and water which freezes around the piling; ice is thus used as construction material.

c. An oil company has "poured" an ice island twenty-six acres in area and thirty feet high. The ice island is capable of supporting a drilling rig with ease.

d. A plan for a barge that sprays water around its sides is being considered by an oil company. The wall of ice thus formed around the barge's perimeter will protect it from ice floes.

EXERCISE 7 *Choose one of the following topic sentences and then write a 100–200 word paragraph supporting it as factually as you can. Do not rely solely on imagination for the facts. Consult outside sources such as books, magazines, and newspapers for information, or else use actual observations and personal experiences.*

1. At the start of a football game the moment of kickoff is especially exciting.
2. Being in love is a nuisance.
3. Being in love is absorbing.
4. Being in love is ecstasy.
5. Exercising violently on a hot day can be dangerous, if not fatal.
6. Cats are independent pets.
7. Major surgery is a shock to the entire body.
8. I believe that the study of mathematics teaches us several habits generally beneficial to anyone.
9. The freedom to dress and groom ourselves as we please enables us to express our tastes and values in very explicit ways.
10. The qualities that make a good fisherman also make a good listener.
11. Being in love is a mixed blessing.
12. The children in the neighborhood thought that Uncle Wilhelm was a very entertaining old man.
13. Smoking my first cigarette at twelve did not result in an enjoyable occasion.
14. To be spoiled is to have unreasonable expectations.
15. Unless it is being done only temporarily as a means to an end, most unskilled, laboring work is discouraging.
16. A number of interesting careers are closed to people who are especially poor in mathematics.
17. A block against mathematics can make that subject seem unnecessarily difficult for us.
18. Of all the colors in nature, green is my favorite.
19. A steady and familiar purr and hum of your automobile engine and its drive train suggests that a number of parts are properly functioning.
20. When we hear that the image of something or somebody is going to be improved, we should be on our guard.
21. Babysitting is a comfortable way to earn money.
22. For many people, writing is a disagreeable task because it is such a solitary activity.

23. Bicycling on country roads can be dangerous for everyone using the roads.
24. Bicycling in the country can be a therapeutic activity.
25. Dancing is one of the oldest and most universal activities of humankind.
26. Singing in choruses or glee clubs is one of the safest and pleasantest ways of expressing yourself.
27. When buying a used car you should constantly keep in mind the old Roman warning *caveat emptor*—let the buyer beware.
28. Summer in many parts of the United States can be as destructive to life and property as winter.
29. Marathon races bring out in the runners some of the most widely-respected human qualities.
30. The career of wide receiver Wes Chandler is a good example of the painful and near-fatal injuries that football players can receive and still keep playing.
31. Trashing up the countryside is a form of selfishness.

32. Your own audience/purpose?

pp 24-26 most imp.

p. 26 → later

Do exercise 8, p. 33 (9 is optional)

Unity

2

Unity is a word used in most books on writing. Defined most simply, unity might be called the *quality of oneness,* a union of related parts that form a harmonious whole. As such, unity is a necessary characteristic of every area of civilized life, from philosohy to music to architecture, sports, engineering, politics, and even cooking. Good writing, too, requires unity of structure, whether that writing takes the form of a novel, an essay, or a single paragraph.

What is unity in writing and how does it work in a paragraph? Often, an effective way to define an object or quality is to begin by showing what it is *not.* The following student paragraph could serve as a case in point:

(1) Despite progress, Navajos still suffer many setbacks. (2) Many Navajos live in beautiful, remote canyons and have organized themselves into about seventy-five clans. (3) They have a basic communication problem with outsiders, and they can't always be understood well enough to be hired. (4) They are years behind the times. (5) Many Navajos still believe in primitive medicine, which has no scientific basis. (6) No single medicine man knows all the rituals needed to cure illness. (7) Many people thus die of strange illnesses. (8) On the other hand, Navajo silvercraft and blanket weaving are two real assets to the Indians. (9) A Navajo blanket will sometimes sell for more than five thousand dollars. (10) People need a balanced diet of meat, vegetables, and carbohydrates. (11) One of the staples of the Navajo diet is fried bread. (12) Such fried, starchy foods are not nutritious. (13) Malnutrition and digestive ailments plague the Navajo. (14) Navajos believe that such diseases happen when a person is out of harmony with nature. (15) In spite of these hardships, the Navajos are one of the most beautiful peoples around, and their entire philosophy is based on a love of beauty.

Whatever we might say about this paragraph, we could not call it organized or unified. Let's examine it in detail.

In the topic sentence, the writer promises to discuss the difficulties or
setbacks faced by the Navajo people of the Southwest. Accordingly, sentences 3, 4, 7, and 13 are focused upon *setbacks* that keep the Navajo from
making progress toward better health and more effective communication
with the world outside the ancestral grounds. But at many points in the
paragraph, the writer wanders from the prescribed subject. Sentence 2,
for example, tells of the beauty of the Navajo habitat and of Navajo organization into clans. Sentences 8 and 9 discuss a successful part of the
Navajo economy. By sentence 10, the writer seems to have forgotten the
promise to describe the plight of the Navajos and begins to discuss human nutritional requirements everywhere. Sentence 14 deals with the
Navajo philosophy of oneness with the natural world. Despite having made
some informed and convincing points about the troubles of the Navajos,
the writer has failed to achieve a oneness of purpose in this paragraph,
and the effort turns out to be unharmonious, scattered in intention.

Fortunately, the writer revised the early paragraph and later in the semester was able to produce the following:

(1) While Navajos have made progress in the past two decades, life for many
is still not easy. (2) Approximately 65,000 of the 133,000 Navajos of the
Southwest speak no English, making the employment problem acute in an
English-speaking economy. (3) As a result, Navajo unemployment stands at
more than sixty percent, and the average yearly income for a Navajo family
is only about $300.00, far below ordinary subsistence levels for the rest of
the country. (4) Navajo health problems are related to economic conditions.
(5) Since they cannot always afford meat and other staples, Navajos must
often do with fried bread, beans, soft drinks, and "junk" foods, hardly a diet
to produce good health. (6) They suffer from intestinal and respiratory diseases which their handful of medicine men are unable to deal with. (7) The
infant death rate per 1,000 live births is 42.3, over three times as high as
the infant mortality rate for other Americans. (8) Technologically, the Navajo are often years behind the times. (9) Many Navajo farmers and shep-
herds still obtain drinking and irrigation water by digging a hole in a dry
stream bed and siphoning off the meager supply that gathers. (10) Despite
these hardships, however, the Navajos are one of the most beautiful of people, and their entire philosophy is based on a love of beauty and on reaching
harmony with nature.

Several characteristics of this revision make it more effective than the
original paragraph. For one thing, the main part of each sentence (subject
and predicate) relates to the controlling idea of the paragraph, *not easy*.
By maintaining contact with the controlling idea, the writer has avoided
skipping around to unrelated subjects that would have distracted the
reader's attention from the major issue of the paragraph.

As a rule, unity is achieved by relating the main part of each supporting sentence directly to the controlling idea of the topic sentence. To more effectively accomplish unity, you might keep asking yourself, "What is my *purpose?* What am I trying to accomplish or prove in this paragraph?" Allow no sentence in the paragraph to deviate from the pattern projected by the topic sentence. If you have an intriguing sentence or an idea that does not relate directly to the controlling idea, suppress the urge to write it down, at least temporarily. Perhaps it can still be used. Later in this chapter you will find out how to use material that is somewhat related to the subject but not strictly unified with the controlling idea of the paragraph.

Main Clause Unity

At this point we will quickly review the difference between a *main* (independent) *clause* and a *subordinate* (dependent) *clause,* because unity depends, for the most part, on main clauses being related to the topic sentence. You probably know that a *clause* is a group of words that contains a subject and a verb (underlined in the following examples, with one line beneath the subject and two beneath the verb):

1. Before Teofilo reached the bridge
2. Seventeen feet high, Roman arches of granite rock marched across the riverbed through the water over to the far bank.
3. As the sound of field artillery became louder
4. Well concealed by the stone, Teofilo expertly attached a dynamite charge to the foot of each arch.
5. If Teofilo gave much thought to the slaves who had designed and built this ancient bridge

The constructions above are clauses, but they are not all main (independent) clauses. Examples 2 and 4 are independent, for they can stand by themselves. But examples 1, 3, and 5 are dependent (subordinate) clauses; the beginning word in each—a *subordinator*—warns you that you are dealing with a construction that cannot stand by itself. Take a perfectly good sentence:

One part of Teofilo Echevarria hated the idea of blowing up the bridge.

Obviously, such a group of words is quite capable of standing alone. But place a subordinator in front of it and see what happens:

Although one part of Teofilo Echevarria hated the idea of blowing up the bridge

What was once an independent clause now needs help from something else. Without help, the clause remains a fragment, a construction that cannot stand by itself.

To return for a moment to Teofilo, let's suppose the topic of your paragraph is Teofilo's determination to destroy the bridge, although another part of him is so awed by the bridge's beauty and antiquity that he can hardly bear to destroy it. Nevertheless, because of loyalty to his comrades and his country, the part that moves him to destroy is heavily weighted against the part that begs him to preserve. The destructive or main idea, then, should be given top billing, that is, placed in the main clause. So you would want to aid the above subordinate clause in the following manner:

> Although one part of Teofilo Echevarria did not want to blow up the bridge, another part of him was totally focused on the concealment, precision, and speed necessary for the job.

Notice that it makes no difference here where the subordinate clause is placed. It can begin or end the sentence. The important point is that the *main* (independent) part of the sentence is the part that proves or supports the controlling idea, and in the above example the main idea expresses Teofilo's commitment to demolishing the bridge. Let's imagine the sort of **TS** (topic sentence) the above construction might help prove:

> Although something in Teofilo's spirit rebelled against the idea, he was now determined to destroy the old Roman bridge over the River Zora.

To prove such a topic sentence, we are not *directly* concerned with Teofilo's conflict, although it makes an interesting minor idea. You needn't abandon that conflict in the paragraph (for it *humanizes* Teofilo), but you must place it out of the way of the real business of the paragraph—his determination to destroy the bridge—as promised in the controlling idea. In short, if you subordinate Teofilo's reluctance to this determination, then you will keep your paragraph unified, with all the main ideas supporting the controlling idea of the **TS**.

None of this means that you can't go another way with Teofilo. Suppose you want to stress his reluctance to blow up the bridge. A change of purpose calls for a revised **TS**:

> Although he appeared determined to set the dynamite charges, Teofilo's spirit rejected the idea of destroying the Roman bridge over the River Zora.

The supporting sentence would simply reverse the priorities of our earlier sentence about Teofilo, by stressing his feelings for preserving the bridge rather than his commitment to destroy it.

As he expertly attached a charge near the foot of an arch, Teofilo began to see in his mind's eye the slaves working on the bridge almost two thousand years ago, the daily commerce that still crossed the bridge, and looking up he was struck by the beauty of the arch soaring above him.

You might remark that the difference between one approach and the other in the Teofilo story is like the difference between saying that his bottle is half-empty and saying that it is half-full. If you stressed the former, you'd be dealing with the negative; if you stressed the latter, you'd be concerned with the positive. Either way, *you* have done the choosing, and now it's up to you to maintain your focus in the main clauses of your supporting sentences. If the information you gather won't support your tentative topic sentence, *then you must modify the* **TS** *to fit the information you have found.* (Later, you will use this same process to develop a thesis for a term paper or a master's thesis or a dissertation or even a scientific theory.)

A note of caution: because good writers usually place minor or subordinate ideas in dependent clauses, don't underestimate the potential that dependent clauses have for generating purpose and power in a sentence, often by making sense out of the independent clause. A case in point: after the black comedian Richard Pryor accidentally set himself on fire in 1980, he worked up a comedy skit based on the frightening experience, in which he asked himself in front of his audience what he learned from the incident. He replied, "When you're on fire and running down the street, people will get out of your way."

Obviously, the main (independent) clause here wouldn't amount to much without the subordinate (dependent) clause.

For another idea of what can happen when a writer gets careless with focus, let's look at a paragraph that was criticized by an instructor for lacking unity. Subjects and verbs of main clauses are underlined.

What is remarkable about the American runner Mary Decker is the range of distances in the races in which she set records in a single year, 1982. (2) First, she won the women's 1,500 meter race at the U.S. Olympic Invitational meet in January 1983. (3) This was done after an injured Achilles tendon had kept her out of competition for over a year-and-a-half. (4) Next, barely a month later, in February, at the *Los Angeles Times* Games she set a new world record of 8 minutes 47.3 seconds in the 3,000 meter race. (5) Also, at the same meeet she ran a new best time of 5 minutes 53.4 seconds in the 2,000 meter. (6) A few days later the track world was amazed as the continent-hopping Ms. Decker showed up at Madison Square Garden and won her race, although she seemed to take in stride her setting a new world record in the indoor mile with a time of 4 minutes 21.47 seconds. (7) A week later she was back on the West Coast, where at the Jack-in-the-Box Invitational indoor track meet in San Diego she ran the same race in 4 minutes 20.5 seconds. (8) Ms. Decker lives in Eugene, Oregon, and it was here where next she lowered the world record in the outdoor 5,000 meter to 15 minutes 8.3 seconds. (9) A month later, she hopped over to Paris, where she became the first woman to run a 4-minute 18.08 second mile outdoors. (10) Then at Oslo <u>she</u> <u>set</u> a new U.S. record of 8 minutes 29.8 seconds in the outdoor 3,000 meter. Returning to Eugene and running the 10,000 meter in 31 minutes 35.3 seconds at the University of Oregon, a new world record in that event, <u>she</u> <u>was</u> ready now to be named amateur sportswoman of the year by the Women's Sports Foundation in October 1982.

Not a bad paragraph, you are probably thinking. And you have a point. The paragraph is, generally, clearly phrased, and it does have plenty of information for developing the controlling idea. Yet if we all agree that the controlling idea is the promise the writer makes to the reader, we have to admit that in this paragraph that promise has not always been kept. For the controlling idea—the range of distances that Mary Decker ran in championship time—is not always directly supported. The facts of her times and the variety of distances in her races are all there, but much of the time they are almost buried in subordinate clauses or turn up, like poor cousins, in other dependent constructions. The main clauses often support some other idea—for instance her resemblance to a whirling dervish or a jet-setter in her rapid continents- and ocean-hopping. You might try checking each of the clauses whose subject and verb are underlined against the following topic sentence:

> In 1982, Mary Decker's traveling must have exhausted her as much as her racing.

Do the main clauses in the last six sentences fit the above topic sentence rather than the paragraph's topic sentence? If so, then obviously we must change the main clause in each of those sentences so that each has an idea that develops the controlling idea of the paragraph's topic sentence. Notice sentence 6: the most important idea here seems to be that the track world is amazed, the next important idea is that they are amazed at Ms. Decker's even showing up, and the least important idea of all is that she set a new world's record in the indoor mile, so buried is this fact in the dependent phrase *setting a new world record.*

Compare the writer's original paragraph with a revised version. Again, subjects and verbs of main clauses have been underlined.

<u>What is remarkable</u> about the American runner Mary Decker <u>is</u> the range of distances at which she set records in a single year, 1982. (2) In January, after an injured Achilles tendon had kept her out of competition for a year-and-a-half, <u>she</u> <u>won</u> the women's U.S. Olympic Invitational 1,500 meters in 4:8.32. (3) At the *Los Angeles Times* Games the following month, <u>she</u> <u>set</u> a world record of 8:47.3 for 3,000 meters. (4) At the same meet, <u>she</u> <u>ran</u> a new personal best of 5:53.4 for 2,000 meters. (5) Within days, to the amazement of the track world, <u>she</u> <u>established</u> a world mark of 4:21.47 in the Wanamaker Mile at Madison Square Garden. (6) <u>She</u> <u>improved</u> that mark to 4:20.5 a week

later at the Jack-in-the-Box Invitational. (7) In her home town of Eugene, she reduced the outdoor 5,000 meter standard to 15:8.3. (8) In Paris, she became the first woman to break 4:20 in the outdoor mile, and at Oslo she ran to a record of 8:29.8 in the 3,000 meter. (9) Returning to Eugene, Decker added a new world 10,000 meter record to her already awesome holdings: 31:35.3. (10) Mary Decker was the fastest American woman in six events, from 800 to 10,000 meters, and was named Amateur Sportswoman of the Year by the Women's Sports Foundation in October 1982.

You might argue that the revised version is not drastically different from its original. And again you would have a point. Actually, all of the same facts and figures have been used to support the topic sentence in the revision. The difference is that in the rewrite the important facts and figures have been repositioned in the main clauses, instead of being placed in the dependent parts of sentences. Additionally, the ideas and facts of less importance in support of the controlling idea have been reduced from main clauses to dependent clauses or even down to dependent phrases, or in one or two instances were omitted entirely.

To test main clause unity in your own writing, you might try underlining the subject and verb in the main clause of each of your supporting sentences, using one line under the subject and two under the verb or predicate. If the independent clause of each sentence relates directly to the controlling idea, you have probably achieved a reasonable degree of unity. Do you remember that "quality of oneness," that "harmonious whole" we made such an issue of at the beginning of this chapter? Well, the revised paragraph on Mary Decker's track achievements begins to move toward that ideal.

Gaining Unity Through Subordination

We have been discussing the concept *subordination* with regard to the example paragraphs above. Subordination might be defined most simply as the *placing of certain ideas in less important positions in relation to the other ideas in the sentence*. A subordinate clause or phrase, like a subordinate rank in military service, is a part that depends on another, more responsible, part for support or direction. A subordinate construction usually has less weight or significance than the part that it helps qualify or modify. Consider the following sentences:

1. Amos Bravo spent about forty minutes on his freshman English theme.
2. Most of that time he was looking out the window at a bluejay in a loquat tree, or listening to the radio, or watching a drag race on television.
3. He got an A+ on his composition.

If you were writing about this incident, which sentence would you want to emphasize as the most significant or important? Most people, of course, would choose sentence 3; it's the climax of this set of incidents as it describes the success of a creative event. Therefore, sentences 1 and 2 are of less weight and import here. If you were faced with the task of fitting all three of these sentences into a single, more sophisticated sentence, how could you arrange them? One possibility might be the following:

> Although Amos Bravo spent only about forty minutes on his freshman English theme and most of that time was looking out the window at a bluejay in a loquat tree, or listening to the radio, or watching a drag race on television, he got an A+ on his composition.

What has happened in this instance with sentences 1 and 2? How have they been positioned in relation to sentence 3? They may be said to have been *subordinated* (placed in a position of less importance) to sentence 3. Sentences 1 and 2 have been blended into a single clause that the writer has made dependent by placing it after a *subordinator (Although)*. By subordinating these two clauses to the more important one, the writer has positioned all these individual ideas in proper relation to one another.

At first glance, you may not think that subordination has much to do with unity. Yet if the writer of the following paragraph had known as much as you now know about subordination, the paragraph probably wouldn't have been penalized for lack of unity:

> (1) As the world's food requirements increase along with the growing population, theorists are discussing means of controlling and domesticating sea creatures. (2) The theories advanced in Arthur C. Clarke's book *The Deep Range* sound like science fiction. (3) Clarke suggests that whales be kept in herds through the use of ultrasonic fences stationed along their migration routes. (4) Clarke's alternative is even more bizarre. (5) He recommeds that killer whales be captured. (6) They could be trained to herd and guard the larger whales. (7) And then there are oysters. (8) Experiments are being conducted in which oysters are raised on columns of empty shells that are attached to wires and suspended from underwater platforms. (9) This keeps the oysters safe from predators that feed on the bottom. (10) Underwater ranches are places to be set aside for marine husbandry. (11) At these places, turtles and other wandering, but nonmigratory, creatures could be fattened for the food market. (12) If even one of the ideas cited above proves feasible, it could supply some of the food needs of a swelling world population.

Not much analysis is needed to see rather quickly that the controlling idea *(means of controlling and domesticating)* is not supported in every sentence that follows it. Sentences 3, 5, 6, 8, 9, and 11 all seem to support the promise, since each of these deals with a situation in which marine life could be domesticated and raised as an eventual source of food for humans. But what about sentences 2, 4, 7, and 10? Should the writer take the easy way out and get rid of these unrelated sentences? In this instance, the writer refused to be defeated by remembering that it is permissible to incorporate in a paragraph material that is not directly related to the topic sentence. The writer simply subordinated the sentences that didn't relate directly to controlling and domesticating sea creatures to those sentences that did. The result is the following revision:

> As the world's food requirements increase along with the growing population, theorists are discussing means of controlling and domesticating sea creatures. (2) In a theory that sounds like science fiction, Arthur C. Clarke, in his book *The Deep Range*, recommends that whales be herded through the use of ultrasonic fences stationed along their migratory routes. (3) As a bizarre alternative, Clarke suggests that killer whales be captured and trained to herd and guard the larger whales. (4) Although the technique is still only in the experimental stage, oysters have been raised on columns of empty shells suspended on wires from underwater platforms to keep them safe from bottom-dwelling predators. (5) On undersea "ranches," turtles and other wandering, nonmigratory marine creatures could be fattened for the food market. (6) If even one of the theories described above proves feasible, it could help fill some of the world's food requirements.

Note the ways in which the revision improves the original:

1. Most important, it focuses all the independent clauses on the controlling idea, making the paragraph unified. (You might try running a check of your own by underlining the subjects and verbs of the main clauses.)
2. Without sacrificing information, it cuts down the number of sentences from twelve to six. Thus it avoids wordiness.
3. It avoids the repetition found in the original paragraph.
4. It smooths the flow of the prose, making the writing less choppy by using certain transitional phrases. (Transition will be discussed later.)

You'll probably admit that subordination was worth trying in the paragraph above. The returns in better prose were worth the investment of time. What resulted was writing that was more "muscular," since the writer compressed the paragraph through subordination. Subordination, then, helps achieve unity, to be sure. In addition, it can help you cut the fat out of your prose, to work your prose into solid bone and muscle. And who wouldn't enjoy being stronger in one way or another?

Note: Do you have any thoughts about the morality of Clarke's proposals? If you have strong feelings about the subject, write a paragraph in which you give the reasons for those feelings.

SUMMARY

1. Unity (the quality of oneness) occurs in a paragraph in which all the sentences of the paragraph relate to the controlling idea and fulfill its "promise."

2. Strict unity is best achieved by relating the main clause of each supporting sentence to the controlling idea of the **TS.**
3. If you want to use in your paragraph ideas that are not directly related to the main idea, you should position these ideas in subordinate clauses or phrases. Then they may be included in the paragraph.
4. To test main clause unity, you should underline the subject and verb of each main clause and check these against the controlling idea of the paragraph.
5. If most of the information you are uncovering takes a direction different from the one the topic sentence points toward, you must modify the topic sentence to fit the facts you are finding. Such a process leaves you open to discovering new ideas and theories and hypotheses.

One last point—when you are honestly satisfied that your proof supports your hypothesis **(TS)**, be firm in advancing your ideas. Remember, the final direction and content of a good piece of writing are governed by the writer's *intention*. At this stage, do not let the subject carry *you* along. You must control *its* direction. In the last analysis, unity is purpose.

EXERCISE 8   *In the paragraph below, circle the number of any sentence that does not prove the controlling idea of the topic sentence.*

(1) When the Indians of the Great Plains killed a buffalo, they used or consumed virtually every inch of the animal. (2) The meat, of course, was the most important commodity, for it provided the Indians with their main source of protein. (3) Two Indians could butcher and dress an entire animal in an hour. (4) The brains and small intestines could not be preserved. (5) They were cooked and eaten on the field immediately after the buffalo had been butchered. (6) The Indians usually roasted the hump and ate it in a communal celebration the night of the hunt. (7) They left the buffalo's heart behind on the plains as a gift to the spirits. (8) The largest portion of the meat was smoked and then eaten over the winter months when game was scarce. (9) Besides food, the buffalo supplied the Indians with tools and utensils. (10) The paunch was used to make cooking vessels and water buckets, while the horn was cut and shaped into spoons, cups, ladles, and knives. (11) Soaps were made from the fat and thread from the sinew. (12) Sewing needles and hide scrapers were formed from the bones. (13) The buffalo was also a source of weapons. (14) Knife sheaths and shields were fashioned out of the rawhide from a bull's neck. (15) These shields were strong enough to repel an arrow or even a spear. (16) Arrowheads were made from the bone and powder flasks from the horn. (17) Although they could make ornaments from the hair and beard of the buffalo, the Indians did not consider these ornaments to be of great impor-

tance. (18) When the white man slaughtered the buffalo, it cost the Indian far more than just a food supply.

EXERCISE 9 *All but one of the sentences in each of the following groups have a common subject and would constitute a unified paragraph. Pick the sentence that does not belong and place the letter of that sentence in the first blank. In the second blank, summarize the topic that unifies the remaining sentences.*

1. a. In May 1358 the peasants of northeastern France (the *Jacquerie*) rose against their masters, burning castles and slaughtering their residents. A month later an army of the nobility and their retainers defeated the *Jacquerie*.
   b. In 1368, tens of thousands of Chinese peasants revolted against the foreign rule of the Mongols and set up the Ming dynasty.
   c. The highly cultivated and artistic Ming dynasty lasted over three hundred years.
   d. In the Peasants' Revolt (1381) triggered by a poll tax, thousands of English peasants, day laborers, and artisans rose against the government and momentarily controlled London, but were defeated and disarmed.
   e. In the fourteenth century there were scattered peasant outbreaks in central Europe and Italy.

_____ _____

2.   (As noted in Joan Didion's book *Salvador*)
   a. Archbishop Romero was killed as he said mass in the Chapel of the Divine Providence Hospital in San Salvador.
   b. More than thirty people were killed while attending Archbishop Romero's funeral in the Metropolitan Cathedral in San Salvador.
   c. More than twenty people were killed on the steps of the Metropolitan Cathedral.
   d. The dead and twitching bodies of the murdered people could be seen on the steps of the cathedral, on television, for the act of carnage was filmed by a CBS team.
   e. Archbishop Romero had not completed the building of the cathedral because he believed that the work of the church should have priority over its material appearance.

_____ _____

3. a. One of the tests undergone by a twelve-year-old male member of the Txukahamei tribe of South America requires the initiate to strike a wasp's nest with his fist and then endure the stings and fever that follow.

b. In another trial, the boy's legs are painfully scarred with razor-sharp fish teeth.

c. Such tests earn young initiates the right to have sexual relations with women within the tribe.

d. Boys are often sent out to raid the camps of rubber tappers' clothing or equipment to be brought back to the tribe. To be caught by the rubber tappers occasionally results in the death or serious injury of the initiate.

e. A Txukahamei initiate must survive naked in the jungle for a month alone and armed only with a knife.

---

4. a. The winged bean, for centuries a source of high protein to Southeast Asians, is tasty, easily processed, and contains up to 37 percent protein.

b. The buffalo gourd, which grows wild in the American Southwest, has seeds containing up to 35 percent protein.

c. The marama bean growing in the Kalahari Desert is tasty when roasted, has as much protein as soybeans, and is as nourishing as the peanut.

d. Many Americans still prefer steak and potatoes and gravy.

e. Black walnuts, easy to grow and only occasionally utilized, are rich in oils, proteins, and minerals.

---

5. a. Thucydides, the Athenian historian, in his essay "The Denudation of Attica" written in the fifth century B.C., laments the methodical destruction of the forests of Greece to build the merchant and naval ships of ancient Greece.

b. As early as the 1100s large landholders in various parts of France, because of their need for charcoal for metal smelting and processing, began to control the uses of their forests.

c. About the same time German provincial governors in the Harz Mountains, for the same reasons, began systemtically regulating the planting and harvesting of the forests.

d. Later the governments of France and England developed policies strictly regulating the uses of their forests especially to ensure a plentiful, domestic supply of timber for the hulls and masts of the wooden sailing ships of their navies.

e. The U.S. government has begun to practice large-scale regulation of the uses of our forests, because wood products are so important in a modern society.

---

6. a. In 1543, Nicholas Copernicus, a Polish astronomer, published a radical theory contending that the planets circle the sun.

b. In 1609, Galileo Galilei used his telescope to discover mountains on the moon and four small stars in the vicinity of Jupiter.

c. Although Galileo was firm in pressing his findings, the Church authorities of the Inquisition used the threat of torture to persuade him to admit that he had "erred."

d. Johannes Kepler, working with the great, but eccentric, Danish astronomer Tycho Brahe, discovered that the planets moved in oval orbits instead of in circles.

e. Sir Isaac Newton used mathematics to propound laws of planetary motion and of gravitational influence. His most famous theory is stated thus: ". . . to every action there is always an equal and opposite, or contrary, reaction."

f. In our time, Albert Einstein used his theory of relativity to explain the universe in terms of curved space and time.

---

7. a. In 1968, the French film maker, Costa-Gavras, found his metier with his movie *Z*, made in Algiers, set in an unidentified Mediterranean country and based on a real case of political assassination in Greece.

b. In 1970, his *L'Aven*, based on the actual trial and execution of Rudolph Slansky in Prague in 1952, depicted the Stalinist terrorism behind the Iron Curtain.

c. His *Etat de Siege* in 1973 was based on the police control of a city and a savage, political kidnapping in an unidentified South American country, aided by the infiltration and subversive activities of U.S. agents.

d. His popular and latest work *Missing*, starring Jack Lemon, won an Academy Award in 1982.

e. In *Missing* a young American disappears in what is apparently Chile at the time of the actual coup (1973) that overthrew the government and murdered President Allende. The movie depicts the savagery of the new police state and the malign influence of the U.S. agents who supported it.

---

8. a. In the *riparian* wildlife communities along California's creeks, snowberry—a member of the honeysuckle family—yields waxy, white berries that are a favorite food source of jays, sparrows, and thrushes. Indians once made cold remedies from its roots.

b. *Riparian* refers to an association of streamside inhabitants, both animal and plant.

c. One of the featured plants along California creeks is the live oak, whose acorns provide an important element in the diets of squirrels and deer.

d. The hollyleaf cherry produces a cherrylike "drupe," which is a favorite food with many birds. Indians once ate the flesh of the berry raw and ground the seeds into a form of flour.

    e. Poison oak, so hazardous to human skin, is a favorite browse of black-tailed deer. Its berries are eaten by a number of birds.

---

9. a. Ancient Samoan navigators who settled the islands of the Pacific would rely on the flight paths of certain birds to reveal the presence of a nearby island.
    b. To inform themselves of their location, the navigators also looked for wave patterns broken by islands.
    c. Without the help of a single instrument, these seafarers settled every inhabitable island in an expanse of ocean larger than the combined areas of North America and Europe.
    d. The ancient mariners found the latitude of a specific island by knowing the island's zenith stars and by steering by them.
    e. The seafarers knew the Pacific bird zones which quartered only certain kinds of birds and would therefore reveal a ship's approximate location. The birds' dawn and dusk flight patterns pointed the way to land.

EXERCISE 10   *Do exactly as you did in the preceding exercise*

1. a. The writer and statesman Archibald MacLeish was awarded two Pulitzer prizes for poetry.
    b. MacLeish was born May 7, 1892, of a prominent family in Glencoe, Illinois, and died April 20, 1982, in Boston, Massachusetts.
    c. He graduated from Harvard Law School and practiced law for three years.
    d. He won a Pulitzer prize for drama with his play in verse *J.B.,* which became a Broadway hit.
    e. He was librarian of Congress from 1939 to 1944, and assistant secretary of state from 1944 to 1945.
    f. He was chairman of the U.S. delegation to the London conference of 1945 that drafted the UNESCO constitution.

---

2. a. The people of medieval Europe built the Gothic cathedrals, which many people think are the most beautifully and inspiringly designed and adorned buildings in the world.
    b. Medieval Europeans contended with the harshness of nature, diseases of epidemic proportions, famine, almost continual warfare, and most of all their own fears, ignorance, and superstitions.

c. Almost every country of medieval Europe established a number of universities, many of which have become famous and are still vigorously alive.

d. The development of the concept or movement known as *humanism* in medieval Europe formed the basis for modern scientific investigation and such modern values and concepts as the political and socio-economic rights of ordinary people everywhere.

e. After the breakup of the Roman Empire, one way or another, according to many scholars, Medieval Europe managed to keep alive such Judaeo-Christian concepts as love, charity, and human brotherhood and such Graeco-Roman ideas as law, mathematics, and a respect for abstract and objective truths as ideals.

---

3. a. In medieval Europe the form of capital punishment for people of the lower classes was usually hanging, and for the upper classes, beheading.

b. In England, traitors were usually partially strangled, then drawn (disemboweled), then quartered (body literally chopped up into four pieces).

c. In France, traitors were pulled apart by powerful workhorses or attached to a large wooden wheel whereupon their principal bones were systematically broken with sledge hammers.

d. Witches and heretics were burnt alive.

e. Petty thievery and misdemeanors were often punished by mutilation and branding, ears, noses and limbs often being cut off.

f. Torture was legally and widely used in medieval Europe to gain confession of crimes.

g. The legal apparatus widely used in medieval Europe was a highly codified and complicated system.

---

4. a. When ace automobile racer Archie Magwirth finished a race at Detroit, Michigan, last year, he had huge blisters on his hands from gripping the wheel so savagely.

b. Magwirth, who is from Leeds, England, broke his left leg in a pileup at the fairgrounds in Reading, Pennsylvania.

c. Three months later at Dayton, Ohio, he was badly burned when the cockpit wiring of his midget auto caught fire.

d. In April of last year, when Magwirth was the leading money winner, he flipped his car at a race in Forth Worth, Texas, and suffered a broken right arm.

e. He would have finished the season driving one-handed, but an appendicitis attack in Waukegan, Illinois, required immediate surgery and prevented him from finishing at all.

---

5. a. Milka Plancic is the first woman to head the government of Yugoslavia or of any other Eastern European country.
   b. On May 16, 1982, the Federal Assembly of Yugoslavia elected her as president of the Federal Executive Council for a four-year term, which made her head of state.
   c. President Plancic was born in November 1924 in Croatia.
   d. In 1941 she graduated from the Senior Administrative School in Zagreb.
   e. According to a French traveler, some Bosnian farmers have their doubts about a woman president.
   f. In 1941 Ms. Plancic joined the Communist Youth Union of Yugoslavia. In 1943 she joined the Yugoslavia Liberation Army and fought as a partisan against the German army of occupation.

---

6. a. The medieval Tuscan rural landscape was usually divided into fields of wheat, groves of olive trees, and grape vineyards, with vegetable gardens around the peasant's house.
   b. The vineyards were carefully tended—pruned, fertilized, and weeded.
   c. The landscape, like Florentine craftsmanship, was a work of art.
   d. The grain fields and olive groves were perfectly cultivated, plowed, and harvested promptly, all weeds and litter carefully used and disposed of.
   e. In the winter and spring, the rains fell softly on the Tuscan countryside, while in the summer and fall the sun's rays shone down like laid-on hands on the ripening crops.
   f. The Tuscan farms made a good profit for *oste* and *contadini* who owned and managed them, and a good living for the *mezzadro*, who did the actual sweating and swinking.

---

7. a. Before the arrival of the Spaniards, the Aztecs in the valley of Mexico painstakingly terraced the sloping land with earthen dikes and stone retaining walls.
   b. Richness of soil for high production was carefully maintained by strict regulation of irrigation and the careful addition of both plant and animal fertilizers.
   c. Irrigation was done in early spring before planting so that the plants

would have a headstart before the early autumnal frosts. Water was led to the terraces by a complex system of ditches, canals and sluice gates.
   d. The lakes in the valley were themselves farmed by a system called chinampa, first used in Lake Chalco.
   e. In the unique chinampa system, swamps were reclaimed by large-scale drainage systems and artificial soil was made by building up mud and swamp plants, resulting in uniquely beautiful and highly productive lake "fields."
   f. At an elevation of 7,000 feet, a relatively small amount of arable land in this Mexican basin provided much of the food for the almost 1.5 million people in the immediate vicinity.

8. a. In 1925, when General Billy Mitchell was convicted of insubordination by a U.S. Army court-martial, the only member of the board who disagreed with the "guilty" verdict was General Douglas MacArthur.
   b. Mitchell had incurred the wrath of powerful officers when he proved in an actual test that a battleship could be sunk by aerial bombing, and he further angered them by telling the press how little foresight the "old-line" brass had.
   c. Just prior to his dramatic demonstration of air power, Mitchell had been quoted as saying, "The General Staff knows as much about the air as a hog does about skating."
   d. The year before his court-martial, Mitchell had publicly predicted with uncanny accuracy the 1941 bombing of Pearl Harbor by the Japanese, who were ostensibly friendly toward us in the 1920s.
   e. Even after he quit the army to avoid being ejected, Mitchell barnstormed around the country speaking on behalf of air power and the need to be prepared.

9. a. "Gloria," sung by Laura Branigan, was in the disco-period top forty songs longer than any other single song since Debbie Reynold's "Tammy."
   b. "Gloria" was sung three times on the Merv Griffin Show.
   c. "Gloria" made number one in November 1982.
   d. Sid Bernstein, once Laura Branigan's manager, is now suing the singer for $15,000,000 for breach of contract.
   e. In January 1983 "Gloria" sales topped one million and it was nominated for a Grammy.

10. a. Samuel von Pufendorf (1632–1694) said that men were not meant to be slaves. Many people of his time disagreed with him, believing that there were natural laws that justified slavery.
b. Von Pufendorf believed in religious freedom and tolerance.
c. His writing foreshadowed some of the ideas expressed by the American Declaration of Independence and the U.S. Constitution.
d. Many of his books were banned by the Austrian government.

EXERCISE 11 *Make a single sentence out of each of the following groups of sentences. The finished sentence should have one main clause and as many subordinate elements as you need to include all the details. Place the most significant element of each group in the main clause of your finished sentence.*

Example

Original: Professor Bloesser firmly believes a good pupil is a busy pupil. Professor Bloesser expects his composition students to do at least three hours of homework for each hour spent in class.

Revision: *Because* he firmly believes that a good pupil is a busy one, Professor Bloesser expects his composition students to do at least three hours of homework for every hour spent in class.

1. The TV series *M*A*S*H* was discontinued by CBS in 1983. That was after eleven years of production. *M*A*S*H* was an enormously popular show.

_____

_____

_____

2. The drive-in movie was once an American institution. Today it is an endangered species.

_____

_____

_____

3. We used to believe that whales were shy creatures in the wild. Now we are learning that they like to come close enough to be petted by humans in a small boat.

_____

_____

_____

4. Iowa occupies only a little over 1 percent of U.S. land area. It contains one-fourth of the nation's top-grade soil. This makes agriculture Iowa's prime industry.

_____

_____

_____

5. Mary Leakey discovered the jaw of a humanlike creature. It was believed to be nearly four million years old. It was discovered at Laetolil. Laetolil is in Africa.

_____

_____

_____

EXERCISE 12   *Combine the short sentences in each of the following support groups into one long sentence. The longer sentence should have a single main clause and as many subordinate clauses and phrases as you need to include all the details. The main clause should support the topic sentence.*

Example

TS: Ernest Hemingway believed that a good outdoorsman/hunter must avoid killing wastefully.

Support: Once Hemingway was hunting. He was hunting big game. It was in Wyoming. He refused to shoot a moose. He had the moose in his sights. He explained that no reasonable man would eat moosemeat when there was elk around.

Revision: While hunting big game in Wyoming once, Hemingway refused to shoot a moose he had in his sights, explaining that no reasonable man would eat moosemeat when there was elk around.

Or: Since he believed no reasonable man would eat moosemeat when there was elk around, Ernest Hemingway once refused to shoot a moose he had in his sights while hunting game in Wyoming.

  1. **TS:**   Hemingway was a fisherman of great strength and determination.

   Support: In 1935 Hemingway was deep sea fishing. It was in the Caribbean off Bimini. He fought a huge hammerhead shark. He fought the shark for hours. He fought the shark until its heart failed. Hemingway hauled it aboard.

Revision: _____

_____

_____

_____

2. **TS:**   Ernest Hemingway could be very hard on friends who failed to live up to a strict code of conduct.

Support: Scott Fitzgerald was a famous author. Fitzgerald was the author of *The Great Gatsby*.
Hemingway accused Fitzgerald of misusing his talent. He accused Fitzgerald of drinking too much. These were vices Hemingway believed could wreck a writer.

Revision: _____

_____

_____

_____

3. **TS:**   Some people took great risks to stay close to Hemingway.

Support: Don Stewart once jokingly promised Hemingway to climb into the bullring and fight. Stewart was thrown twice. He suffered several broken ribs. Stewart kept maintaining that he didn't want to "disappoint Ernie."

Revision: _____

_____

_____

_____

4. **TS:**   Hemingway could be a superstitious man.

Support: He often claimed to be a rationalist. He claimed to be a tough rationalist. He believed it to be "very bad luck" to work on Sunday. He believed that one might become ill if he slept with moonlight on his face. Both were jinxes he had faith in most of his adult life.

Revision: _____

_____

_____

_____

5. **TS:**   Most of the time whatever Hemingway wanted, he got.

Support: Evan Shipman owned a painting Hemingway admired greatly. Shipman loved the painting. Shipman sold the painting to Hemingway. Shipman sold the painting at a great bargain. He was hoping to win Hemingway's approval.

Revision: _____

_____

_____

_____

6. **TS:** Hemingway's capacity to hold his liquor was legendary.

Support: He didn't exactly engage in a drinking contest every day. He once downed sixteen frozen daiquiris. Each daiquiri contained four ounces of rum. Hemingway walked home afterwards. He read all night.

Revision: _____

_____

_____

_____

7. **TS:** When angered by the critics, Hemingway on occasion could take some pretty direct action.

Support: Max Eastman unfavorably reviewed Hemingway's *Death in the Afternoon*. It was in an article entitled "Bull in the Afternoon." Afterwards, Hemingway struck Eastman in the face with a copy of the review. Hemingway wrestled the critic to the floor. Hemingway was leaving little doubt about his sensitivity to professional criticism.

Revision: _____

_____

_____

_____

8. **TS:** Hemingway believed a serious writer would suffer for violating his own literary standards.

Support: A fellow writer "twisted" a story to make it more salable to an expensive magazine. Hemingway told his friend that this was "whoring." He said such practice would ruin a person's talent. Hemingway added that "formula writing" was for amateurs.

Revision: _____

_____

_____

_____

9. **TS:** Hemingway was often a man of immense charm.

   Support: His first wife Hadley once made a statement. She was always a fair person. She said, "He was the kind of man to whom men, women, children, and dogs were attracted. It was something." She said this years after the breakup of their marriage.

   Revision: _____

   _____

   _____

   _____

10. **TS:** Hemingway was convinced that writing was a lonely and necessarily solitary occupation.

    Support: Hemingway once made a comment. He said, "A writer is an outlier like a Gypsy." He added that "to write straight honest prose on human beings" is the world's hardest job.

    Revision: _____

    _____

    _____

    _____

EXERCISE 13   *Do exactly as you did in the preceding exercise.*

1. **TS:** After a voyage filled with hardships, Columbus's 1493 homecoming was threatened by a final danger.

   Support: Columbus was two days from port. The port was Lisbon. Lisbon is in Portugal. An enormous storm struck the *Nina.* The storm ripped all but one of her sails to shreds.

   Revision: _____

   _____

   _____

   _____

2. **TS:** In Barcelona, Columbus triumphantly displayed the rarities he had brought home.

   Support: Columbus went riding at the head of a great procession. Columbus was followed by six costumed Indians. The Indians were carrying brightly colored parrots in cages. They carried golden masks. None of these wonders had ever been seen in Spain before.

   Revision: _____

   _____

3. **TS:** Following the first voyage, King Ferdinand and Queen Isabella rewarded Columbus handsomely.

   Support: The Spanish king and queen had been at first skeptical of Columbus. Columbus was a foreigner. Now they gave him the title "Admiral of the Ocean Sea." Along with the title, they gave him estates and royalties. In these ways they acknowledged his bravery and vision.

   Revision: _____

   _____

   _____

4. **TS:** Columbus's failure to reach the Orient was the result of his miscalculation about the earth's size.

   Support: Most educated men of the day knew the earth was round. Columbus knew the earth was round. He thought it was only about 16,000 miles in circumference. This is a distance about 40 percent short of the actual circumference.

   Revision: _____

   _____

   _____

5. **TS:** During his third voyage, Columbus paid the price for poor administrative judgment.

   Support: Columbus hanged seven rebels at Santo Domingo. The king's visiting administrator was Francisco de Bobadilla. Bobadilla put Columbus in irons. He sent Columbus back home to Spain in disgrace.

   Revision: _____

   _____

   _____

6. **TS:** Not all the Indians Columbus met in the New World were friendly.

   Support: Dominica is an island. It is southeast of Puerto Rico. Columbus encountered fierce cannibals on Dominica. They were called Caribs. They were slave-raiding warriors.

Revision: _____

_____

_____

_____

7. **TS:**   Despite his own dissatisfaction with it, Columbus's third voyage yielded a find of great value to Spain.

  Support: Columbus was very disappointed with the results of the voyage. He discovered an island. The Indians called it "Jamayca." It is one of the most beautiful islands in the Indies.

  Revision: _____

_____

_____

8. **TS:**   Despite his early success, Columbus ended his career as a man who was scorned and ignored.

  Support: He made four voyages. The last ended in 1505. After this voyage the court removed Columbus's titles. They sent no one to Columbus's deathbed. His loyal shipmates were gathered there to pay their last respects.

  Revision: _____

_____

_____

9. **TS:**   Even as he lay dying, Columbus settled his personal obligations.

  Support: Columbus had a mistress. Her name was Beatriz Enriquez de Harana. Columbus asked his son Diego to see that Beatriz was "given enough to live comfortably."

  Revision: _____

_____

_____

EXERCISE 14   *Read each of the following paragraphs for unity. After deciding what the main (or controlling) idea of the topic sentence is, check the independent clause of each subsequent sentence against that controlling idea. If you find sentences that are not directly related,*

1. (1) Although the Multnomah Beavers' offensive tackle, Reinhold von Pufendorf, is well muscled, his size alone would make him an extraordinarily powerful offensive weapon. (2) His charge is as quick and hard as a buffalo's, even though he is 7 feet 2 inches tall and weighs 410 pounds stripped down for a shower. (3) "Animal" McGarrity is one of the toughest and biggest defensive ends in the league. (4) He says that you would have a little better chance to get around "Puf" if you could *see* around him. (5) If the Beaver quarterback Lem Menafee had sense enough to get behind Pufendorf's body and *stay* there, he would have at least fifteen to thirty seconds to get his pass away. (6) Even though von Pufendorf's size is usually a great asset, in a game against the Helena Mountaineers, two defensive linemen dove at his shoulders; temporarily off balance the enormous tackle fell back, landing on top of Menafee's body. (7) Although Lem Menafee is not known for mental quickness, he has never forgotten that day. (8) Pufendorf is not savage either on or off the field. (9) "Curley" Grimes, sports editor of the *Multnomah Beacon*, commenting on his lack of ferocity said, "So what? No one expects a bridge abutment to be ferocious, either. (10) 'Puf' is such a nice guy that he can't resist buying ice cream cones for little kids." (11) Coach Waldo Pilley of the Puget Sound Vikings says, "To hell with his ice cream cones. (12) All I know is that when we play the Beavers we have to make up special plays because of his size." (13) His manager, Shorty di Donato, says, "Although he weighs 410 pounds, he is such a 100 percent awesome guy that in every way he's worth a thousand dollars per pound per year to his club."

2. (1) Aside from their reputation for ferocity, sharks benefit humans in many ways. (2) Sharkskin has a tensile strength of 7,000 pounds per square inch. (3) Sharkskin produces highly durable shoes, belts, and pocketbooks. (4) Such items will wear nearly indefinitely. (5) Shark liver oil is not easily obtainable. (6) It is widely used for tempering steel, making soaps and cosmetics, and producing high-grade lubricant. (7) The texture of shark flesh makes it easy to dry and pulverize. (8) Shark meal is a readily derived food-fortifier for poultry and livestock. (9) It also makes good fertilizer. (10) It is inexpensive enough to be practical. (11) Shark meat is not a popular entree in the United States. (12) In many places, it is a nutritious food source. (13) It is higher in protein than oysters, salmon, milk, or eggs. (14) There is an unlikely use to which shark meat is put. (15) It produces flour. (16) The flour is more nutritious and less expensive than grain flour. (17) These uses establish the shark as more of a boon than a menace to humanity.

3. (1) M. Diana Delacy, a young assistant professor of English, is unsparing in her criticism of graduate students. (2) Dr. Delacy teaches at

Brookdale University of Lodi, California. (3) She described one graduate student's classroom presentation as "a skillful song and dance." (4) Another student had been teaching in the public schools for six years. (5) Dr. Delacy evaluated him with the statement, "The superficiality of his paper on Steinbeck was exceeded only by the shallowness of his presentation of the subject to the class." (6) She added, "For that matter, Steinbeck is shallow, too." (7) A third student was a young woman. (8) Her paper dealt with the subordinate role of women in nineteenth-century English literature. (9) Professor Delacy gave the paper a C. (10) She argued that the thesis was untenable and the whole paper thus invalid. (11) Dr. Delacy, who received her Ph.D. from a prestigious university, is fond of saying, "Grad students here at Brookdale would have lasted a week at Stanford. So did Steinbeck."

All important

Coherence

3

As we have been insisting, unity is a basic structural characteristic of good writing. As such, it must be present in any piece of prose worth reading. However, unity alone—without the help of certain other qualities—cannot ensure a successful paragraph. Consider the following example:

> (1) Shakespeare's Richard III is one of history's meanest villains. (2) He had his brother Clarence killed. (3) Clarence stood in Richard's way to the throne. (4) Richard had him drowned in a huge cask of wine. (5) He hired assassins to kill his two little nephews. (6) The assassins smothered the little princes in their beds. (7) Richard killed his own right-hand man, the Duke of Buckingham. (8) Buckingham had already had enough of Richard and his bloody ways. (9) Richard III was ruthless. (10) He gave the word "villain" new meaning.

This paragraph certainly has unity—all the facts confirm King Richard's ruthlessness. But in this case, unity alone is not enough to make the writing good. The prose is choppy and abrupt; there are no transitions between individual sentences. The paragraph seems to need some words or phrases or signals to ease the movement of the prose and to make the separate facts stick together. This quality, which is present when individual elements stick together, is called *coherence*—a kind of inner logic. It's the companion of unity. If unity is the trunk, or skeleton, upon which the ideas are positioned, coherence is the connective tissue that joins the ideas to one another.

As you remember, unity deals with the relationship between the topic sentence and each of the sentences that follow. Coherence involves the relationship that occurs from sentence to sentence *within* the paragraph.

These sentences must flow together, must be woven together like a fine piece of fabric. We don't expect to find snags, tears, and protruding threads in an expensive piece of cloth. Similarly, good prose should be free of awkward sentences and bumps in the writing. Consider the following paragraph, which we will gradually alter and expand as we dicsuss various ways to gain coherence:

> (1) All paths once led upwards for faith-healer Emma Lavinia Hopewell, but in the past fifteen months she has been running into problems at every turn. (2) The family of a man Emma claimed to have cured of bone cancer won a three million dollar legal suit. (3) Hopewell ordered the family's father to "stop medicating and start meditating." (4) The man died. (5) Hopewell has been charged with fraudulent soliciting of funds. (6) It was alleged that money collected to finance the "City of God" medical facility was used for vacations for Hopewell and the staff at Holiness Pentecostal Temple. (7) Hopewell declared bankruptcy. (8) Her personal earnings have been estimated at one million dollars yearly. (9) Hopewell was criticized by members of the "Children of the Flame" for appearing among the ten best-dressed women in America. (10) Followers were outraged when she signed to star in a Hollywood religious epic. (11) People said it was hard to revere a woman who played a "painted Jezebel" on wide-screen cinemascope. (12) Not all her disciples were angry. (13) One said, "Why criticize her for clothes and cars? She's the prophetess of a first-class God, and He would want His Handmaiden to travel first-class—all the way!"

The writer of this paragraph about Emma Lavinia Hopewell has taken the trouble to get the facts and has unified these facts—facts that deal consistently with the difficulties Emma and her "children" have encountered. However, like the previous writer, this one also undermines the effectiveness of what should have been a fine paragraph. The sentences bump along in a staccato way, when their progress could have been smoothed out with a little effort. The writer loses ease and connectedness by neglecting coherence. You yourself can achieve coherence in a number of ways.

Transition

One of the most convenient ways of smoothing gaps in prose is through *transition,* a term that comes from the Latin *transire,* meaning "to go over or across." Most people would probably agree that it's more pleasant—and much safer—to cross canyons by bridges than by trying to leap across, as motorcyclist Evel Kneivel once attempted to do at Snake River Canyon. Like bridges, transitions open into two directions at the same time—forward to where the writer intends to go and backward to where the writer has been. Transitions are most often achieved by single words or short phrases that can generally be positioned almost anywhere in a sentence. The following transitional words and phrases occur most frequently in writing:

To signal an addition:	and, furthermore, besides, next, moreover, in addition, again, also, similarly, too, finally, second, subsequently, ultimately, last
To signal an example or illustration:	for example, thus, for instance, that is, namely, apparently, evidently
To signal a contrast or alternative:	but, or, not, yet, still, however, nevertheless, on the contrary, on the other hand, conversely
To signal a conclusion:	therefore, thus, then, in conclusion, consequently, as a result, in other words, accordingly, finally

Let us see if the paragraph on Emma Lavinia Hopewell might be improved by the inclusion of some transitonal phrases.

(1) All paths once led upwards for faith-healer Emma Lavinia Hopewell, but in the past fifteen months she has been running into problems at every turn. (2) *For example*, the family of a man Emma claimed to have cured of bone cancer won a three million dollar legal suit. (3) Hopewell *apparently* ordered the family's father to "stop medicating and start meditating." (4) The man died. (5) Hopewell *also* has been charged with fraudulent soliciting of funds. (6) It was alleged that money collected to finance the "City of God" medical facility was used for vacations for Hopewell and the staff at Holiness Pentecostal Temple. (7) Hopewll declared bankruptcy. (8) *Yet* her personal earnings have been estimated at one million dollars yearly. (9) Hopewell was criticized by members of the "Children of the Flame" for appearing among the ten best-dressed women in America. (1) Followers were *further* outraged when she signed to star in a Hollywood religious epic. (11) People said it was hard to revere a woman who played "a painted Jezebel" on wide-screen cinemascope. (12) Not all her disciples were angry, *however*. (13) *In fact*, one said, "Why criticize her for clothes and cars? She's the prophetess of a first-class God, and He would want His Handmaiden to travel first-class—all the way!"

Repetition

An equally important though less obvious method of achieving coherence is through repetition of and reference to key words in the paragraph. Often these words are pronouns, but they may be nouns and sometimes adjectives as well. For our purposes, nouns and pronouns are probably best. You can no doubt see the reason why pronouns—words that are "stand-ins" for nouns—are particularly useful in linking ideas from sentence to sentence. They establish a pattern of identity through the paragraph by referring back to nouns or to other pronouns that precede them. These words—in their modest way—keep the reader's attention focused continuously on the people, objects, or ideas that are the subject of the paragraph. Consider whether the coherence of our sample paragraph is further improved by the following repetition of key terms or substitutes for those key terms:

(1 All paths once led upwards for faith-healer Emma Lavinia Hopewell, but in the past fifteen months *she* has been running into problems at every turn. (2) For example, the family of a man *whom* Emma claimed *she* cured of bone cancer won a three million dollar legal suit against *her*. (3) Hopewell apparently ordered *their* father to "stop medicating and start meditating." (4) The man died. (5) Hopewell also has been charged with fraudulent soliciting of funds. (6) It was alleged that money collected to finance *her* "City of God" medical facility was used for vacations for Hopewell and *her* staff at Holiness Pentecostal Temple. (7) Hopewell declared bankruptcy. (8) Yet *her* personal earnings have been estimated at one million dollars yearly. (9) Hopewell was criticized by members of *her* "Children of the Flame" for appearing among the ten best-dressed women in America. (10) Followers were further outraged when *she* signed to star in a Hollywood religious epic. (11) *They* said it was hard to revere a woman who played a "painted Jezebel" on wide-screen cinemascope. (12) Not all *her* disciples were angry, however. (13) In fact, one said, "Why criticize *her* for clothes and cars? *She's* the prophetess of a first-class God, and *He* would want *His* Handmaiden to travel first-class—all the way!"

Modification

Modification is another method of improving coherence in prose. To modify something means to alter it in some significant respect. The enthusiast who modifies a stock-car engine, for instance, changes the standard specifications of that engine in such a way that it has more power and thus can produce greater speed. In modifying prose, a writer tries to give it more power by adding supplemental details to individual sentences. Most often, these details improve the quality of the writing by contributing *specific* pieces of information that the reader is interested in knowing. Modifiers answer such questions as *who, how, when, where, why,* and *under what circumstances.*

Modifiers come in many varieties. They can take the form of single words, such as adjectives or adverbs:

Adjective:	a *devout* follower
Adverb:	a *critically* important sermon
Adjectival past participle:	a *painted* woman

These modifiers tend to affect the power of the nouns they modify. The modifier in the first instance announces that the disciple is not simply a follower but a *worshipful* one. In the second example, the *sermon* becomes something more than just a speech; it becomes *crucial* following modification. In the third example, the woman becomes a gaudy, even illicit, one.

Modification can also be accomplished with phrases. The three most common types of modifying phrases are:

A. Past participial:
1. *Abandoned by his parents,* the child was forced to develop independence.
2. The child *abandoned by her parents* grew up to head a religious movement.

B. Present participial:
1. *Grasping the possibility of unlimited revenues,* the prophetess taxed every person in the faith.

C. Prepositional:
1. *After declaring bankruptcy,* the "Children of the Flame" decided to change their address.
2. The "Children of the Flame," *upon declaring bankruptcy,* decided to leave town.
3. The "Children of the Flame" decided to leave town *after losing a lawsuit.*

Note that the modifying phrases used above provide information about the group's activities. That is, the phrases *modify* the original situation by telling *who* in the examples under A, *how* in the example under B, and *when* in the examples under C. Note also that all these modifiers can be used at several places in the sentence.

Of the three types of phrases, the prepositional phrase is the most immediately useful and versatile. It conveys a wide range of information without cluttering up the sentence.

> The "Children of the Flame" ran their operation (at an office) (in their lavish temple) (in Amarillo, Texas.)

In the above example, the three successive prepositional phrases tell *where* the group operated. In the following sentence, prepositional phrases tell *when, why, how,* and *where:*

> *In August,* the "Children of the Flame," *in order to reach the faithful,* distributed leaflets *by mail throughout the U.S.*

Let us look at our sample paragraph once more to determine if adding some modification will enhance its coherence:

(1) All paths once led upwards for faith-healer Emma Lavinia Hopewell, but in the past fifteen months she has been running into problems at every turn. (2) For example, the family of a man whom Emma claimed she cured of bone cancer won a three million dollar legal suit against her. (3) *During a revival meeting in Tallahassee*, Hopewell apparently ordered their father to "stop medicating and start meditating." (4) The man died. (5) *To make matters worse*, Hopewell also has been charged with fraudulent soliciting of funds. (6) It was alleged that money collected to finance her "City of God" medical facility was used for vacations for Hopewell and her staff at Holiness Pentecostal Temple *in Amarillo*. (7) Hopewell declared bankruptcy. (8) Yet her personal earnings have been estimated at one million dollars yearly. (9) Hopewell was criticized by members of her "Children of the Flame" for appearing among the ten best-dressed women in America. (10) Followers were further outraged when she signed to star in a Hollywood religious epic. (11) They said it was hard to revere a woman who played a "painted Jezebel" on wide-screen cinemascope. (12) Not all her disciples were angry, however. (13) *On the Phil Donahue TV show*, one said, "Why criticize her for clothes and cars? She's the prophetess of a first-class God, and He would want His Handmaiden to travel first-class—all the way!"

Logical Order

Modification can also be put to special uses in the paragraph. One such use lies in establishing *logical order* in the paragraph or essay. Logical order helps to keep writing coherent because it ties the ideas to a distinct structure: time, space, or cause/effect, to mention a few possibilities. Before we take leave of Emma Hopewell and her problems, let's look at the paragraph for one last time; now we will establish a *chronological* (time) order by using certain kinds of modifications:

(1) All paths once led upwards for faith-healer Emma Lavinia Hopewell, but in the past fifteen months she has been running into problems at every turn. (2) For example, the family of a man whom Emma claimed she cured of bone cancer *recently* won a three million dollar legal suit against her. (3) During a revival meeting in Tallahassee *last March*, Hopewell apparently ordered their father to "stop medicating and start meditating." (4) *Soon afterwards*, the man died. (5) To make matters worse, Hopewell also has been charged with fraudulent soliciting of funds. (6) It was alleged that money collected to finance her "City of God" medical facility was used for vacations *last summer* for Hopewell and her staff at Holiness Pentecostal Temple in Amarillo. (7) Hopewell *promptly* declared bankruptcy. (8) Yet her personal earnings have been estimated at one million dollars yearly. (9) Hopewell was criticized by members of her "Children of the Flame" for appearing among the ten best-dressed women in America. (10) *At Christmas* followers were further outraged when she signed to star in a Hollywood religious epic. (11) They said it was hard to revere a woman who played a "painted Jeze-

bel" on wide-screen cinemascope. (12) Not all her disciples were angry, however. (13) On the Phil Donahue TV show *last week*, one said, "Why criticize her for clothes and cars? She's the prophetess of a first-class God, and He would want His Handmaiden to travel first-class—all the way!"

You may be likely to object at this point that the paragraph is "overdone." Perhaps it is. But if there is exaggeration here, it is meant to illustrate those subtleties in writing that lie hidden within the texture of the prose. These modifications aren't supposed to stand out, since good writing doesn't call attention to itself but rather to the subject it treats. Yet you must deliberately try to see how these devices work before you can employ them yourself.

SUMMARY

1. Coherence eases the movement of prose and makes separate facts stick together.
2. Transition, one of the most convenient ways of smoothing gaps in prose, is often achieved by single words and phrases (like *and, furthermore, for example, but, therefore, finally,* and so on) that can be positioned almost anywhere in a sentence.
3. Repetition of pronouns, nouns, and adjectives establishes a pattern of identity throughout at paragraph by keeping the readers' attention focused on the people, objects, or ideas that are the subject of the paragraph.
4. Modification improves coherence by adding details that answer such questions as *who, how, when, where, why,* and *under what circumstances.*
5. Logical order ties ideas presented in a paragraph to a distinct order: time, space, or cause and effect, to mention a few possibilities.

EXERCISE 15   *After reading the following paragraph, answer the multiple choice questions at the end of the selection. When required to fill in blanks within the paragraph, choose the appropriate answer from the list given in the multiple choice section.*

(1) Experts and laymen alike have put forward various theories to try to explain the black athlete's apparent predominance in U.S. sports. (2) One popular notion attributes black athletic prowess to the constrained social position of black Americans. (3) Suggests Morehouse College sociologist Corrie Hope, for example, "I'm afraid that being successful in sports will remain for a long time the surest way out of the ghetto." (4) In differentiating between post-collegiate options open to whites and blacks, NFL receiver Paul Warfield ratifies Hope's position by noting that "For the white

athlete, the alternatives have obviously been greater. (5) He doesn't have to channel his energies into one particular area." (6) Another school of thought subscribes to reasons that are nearly anthropological. (7) Baltimore Colt end John Mackey says, "When they turn loose African athletes who have been chasing, say, cheetahs, they will rewrite the record books." (8) From a more clinical perspective, Alvin Poussaint, a black physician and psychiatrist from Harvard, maintains that the selectivity of slavery insured that only the best came to the New World. (9) "First of all," asserts Dr. Poussaint, "they selected for slavery only those with a lot of brawn and the ability to work hard. . . . Second, only the strongest survived the long voyage." (10) In the last analysis, perhaps the most prevalent—if controversial—rationale behind black athletic excellence is the idea of black physical superiority. (11) In pioneer anthropometric studies conducted in the 1920s, Dr. Eleanor Metheny discovered that blacks generally had, in the makeup of their arms and legs, a superior length, musculature, and leverage, all of which lent them an advantage in sprinting and jumping. (12) Dr. Metheny found, _____, that blacks had longer legs in proportion to their body length and that their thighs—though shorter than their calves—were more powerfully muscled than the thighs of white competitors. (13) Whatever may be the cause of black athletic potency, tennis great Arthur Ashe feels that it has been overplayed to the detriment of academic and professional aspiration among black youth. (14) Ashe states his position to his fellow blacks convincingly: (15) "We need to pull over, fill up at the library and speed away to Congress and the Supreme Court, the unions and the business world."

1. In sentence 4, the phrase "In differentiating between post-collegiate options open to whites and blacks" is an example of:
   a. transition
   b. modification
   c. repetition
   d. logical order

2. In sentence 5, the opening "He" *ultimately* refers back to:
   a. Paul Warfield in sentence 4
   b. Corrie Hope in sentences 3
   c. "whites" in sentence 4
   d. "blacks" in sentence 4
   e. "white athlete" in sentence 4

3. Which of the following transitions best fits the blank in sentence 12:
   a. nevertheless
   b. however
   c. consequently
   d. moreover
   e. conversely

4. In sentence 3, the expression "for example" is an instance of:
   a. transition
   b. repetition
   c. modification
   d. subordination

5. Which of the following best describes the type of logical order employed in the paragraph?
   a. time
   b. space
   c. degree: least prevalent to most prevalent
   d. degree: least controversial to most controversial
   e. a and b above
   f. c and d above

6. In sentence 13, in the clause, "Arthur Ashe feels that it has been overplayed," the "it" *ultimately* refers back to:
   a. "athletic potency" in sentence 13
   b. "cause" in sentence 13
   c. "black physical superiority" in sentence 10
   d. "athletic prowess" in sentence 2
   e. "black predominance" in sentence 1

7. In sentence 8, the phrase "From a more clinical perspective" is an example of:
   a. transition
   b. repetition
   c. modification
   d. logical order

8. Although the paragraph focuses on a single topic, it seems to treat several divisions of that topic. The sentences that mark these divisions are:
   a. 3, 4, and 8
   b. 2, 6, and 10
   c. 3, 6, and 13
   d. 5, 8, and 11

9. In sequence, the writer explores the following theories about black excellence in sports:
   a. political, literary, psychological
   b. sociological, anthropological, physical
   c. historical, mathematical, economic
   d. physical, intellectual, biological

10. Each of the sentences that divide the paragraph into sections tends to do which of the following:
    a. it announces a new phase of the subject
    b. it looks back at what the writer has just said

c. it looks forward to what the writer intends to say next

d. it conveys a change in the degree or status of the information

e. all of the above

The kind of sentence being pointed out in questions 8 and 10 is an example of what, in a later chapter, we call *primary support*. It is an important kind of sentence because it functions in two ways: (1) to maintain the unity of the paragraph by dividing the main idea in a logical and focused way, and (2) to strengthen the coherence of the writing, particularly at strategic places in the paragraph. Notice that each of the primary-support sentences (2, 6, and 10) closes out a stage of discussion and focuses upon a new facet of the subject. Thus, it is a pivotal sentence. In performing double duty, a primary-support sentence functions to link together the concepts of unity and coherence.

You'll remember that at the beginning of this chapter we saw examples of writing that had unity but lacked coherence. Such work is possible. Nevertheless, no capable writer would ever be guilty of lacking either quality, or both, for the human mind tends to seek structure—to think in ways that are unified and coherent. Unity and coherence go together— like Tweedledum and Tweedledee, ham and eggs, Batman and Robin, or Romeo and Juliet—you can't have one without the other.

EXERCISE 16   *Fill in each blank with the transitional expression that best expresses the logical relationship between the sentences.*

1. In his rookie year, British auto racer Archie Magwirth won the Daytona 500, the Indianapolis 500, and the Laguna Seca race in California, _____ within two short years Magwirth finished out of the money in every major race, crashed his car at Palm Beach, and withdrew from several major races.

2. Sir Adrian Hawkins holds the record for sailing farther than any lone mariner without sighting land; he is a champion polo player and an Olympic-calibre skeet shooter. _____, he has swum the Hellespont between European and Asiatic Turkey, like Lord Byron before him.

3. In the thirties, forties, and fifties, there was one woman, and one woman alone, who captured the admiration of people of all classes and ethnic backgrounds, _____, Eleanor Roosevelt.

4. In 1940, John Steinbeck was attacked by special interest groups who thought *The Grapes of Wrath* was an immoral, nasty novel that falsely characterized Oklahomans in a derogatory manner. Steinbeck had faith in the honesty of his book, _____, and he lived to see it become an American classic.

5. Composer Jakob Frokmann tried every year for ten years to get the San Francisco Opera to perform his *Flight from Jaffa* or his dramatic

legend entitled *The Fall of the Mongol*. _____ this spring San Francisco agreed to perform Frokmann.

6. Soviet writer Georgi Kalishnikov has been "detained" by the KGB, subjected to harrassment, and had his apartment searched several times. It is not surprising, _____, that Kalishnikov has become slightly defensive.

7. Margaret Mead's anthropological theories, introduced in *Coming of Age in Samoa*, gained a tremendous following in universities for four decades. New Zealander Derek Freeman, _____, has recently seriously disputed the validity of Mead's major claims.

8. The Hacketts' son Gregory had suffered for several years from a lung condition that defied conventional means of therapy. In desperation, they _____ tried the Mayo Clinic, which located and treated the problem.

9. Sir Ronald Peter-Hillyard of Sydney saw the America's Cup narrowly elude him on five occasions. _____ he can hardly be faulted for feeling apprehensive about his boat's chance of winning this year.

10. Chrysler's chairman Lee Iacocca proved in 1983 that energy and a commitment to quality could help pay back the huge loan the government extended his company. _____ it remains to be seen whether he can help keep Chrysler—let alone the American auto industry—financially solvent over the longer haul.

EXERCISE 17 *Sometimes the sentences in a paragraph are "glued" together so well that even when their order is deliberately scrambled, as it is below, you can rearrange them as they were in the original. Indicate the correct order of the sentences in the blank below. Circle the signals that do the "gluing" job.*

1. (a) Others extend their bat at both arms' length above their heads then lower the bat behind their necks as if doing a stretching exercise. (b) Many batters use consistent rituals aimed at bringing them luck at the plate. (c) Some batters adjust their batting helmet, then tap their spikes with their bat, as if to dislodge caked dirt. (d) And yet others spit into their palms, then carefully rub the mixture into the wood of their bat handle. (e) Still others, before stepping into the box, unwrap and readjust their batting glove after every pitch, a time-consuming process that annoys pitchers.

    Correct order: __b c a e d_____

2. (a) Finally, however, the International Whaling Commission has agreed to a five-year moratorium on killing whales, effective in 1986. (b) Even before the birth of Christ, Eskimos on ice floes hunted small whales during migrations. (c) In the Bible Jonah undergoes death and trans-

figuration in the belly of a whale. (d) Since ancient times men have had a close relationship with whales, but it has changed radically in the last few years. (e) Before Leif the Lucky sailed to America in A.D. 1000, Basque seamen fearlessly hunted whales from small boats. (f) But now people take cruises to study and play with whales. (g) In the 1800s Captain Ahab hunted Moby Dick, and the enormous white whale became a symbolic object of man's tragic compulsion to destroy what he himself cannot create. (h) Further, there is worldwide protest against Russian and Japanese whalers who, using the latest technology including explosive harpoons, continue to hunt whales.

Correct order: _____

3. (a) Realizing that Paris was a "closed shop," Michelle emigrated to New York, where she worked as a designer for Malcolm Gutter and Company, a clothing firm. (b) Before a year was up, Michelle was a designer for *Rive Gauche;* some of her creations drew the attention of the New York market, who liked the "elegant simplicity" of her style. (c) Selling jewelry, handbags, and small leather goods—as well as her own creations—she soon made a name for *Michelle, Ltd.* by shipping clothes to Italy and France. (d) When Michelle Fanesse was only ten, she remarked, "I will always get what I want." (e) Today, Princess Michelle de Brantes can boast of a dress empire that allows her to fulfill her early statement that she would get what she aimed for. (f) When she graduated from the Sorbonne in Paris, she got a job merchandising dresses for *Rive Gauche*, an exclusive Paris clothier. (g) By last year, Michelle had built a $15 million international enterprise, selling over 15,000 dresses per week, both in the United States and abroad.

Correct order: _____

EXERCISE 18   *Do exactly as you did in the preceding exercise.*

1. (a) Ancient Egyptian plowmen built clay houses molded out of Nile mud; they stayed cool in the heat of the delta. (b) Throughout history, builders have used virtually every known material in constructing human shelter. (c) Renaissance Englishmen in 1550 used the abundant wood to construct large "Tudor" homes with straw-thatched roofs. (d) Neanderthal man built reed huts on stilts in Swiss lakes—convenient for fishing and crabbing. (e) In medieval Italy, homes were built from native stone—heavy masonry that had strong insulation properties. (f) Scientists predict that on distant planets, humans will eventually house entire communities under giant, atmosphere-preserving geodesic "astrodomes." (g) Today, synthetic, as well as natural, materials go into skyscrapers and individual dwellings. (h) The early colonists to America found some Indian tribes living in "quonset" huts, domed struc-

tures made of a framework of supple wood arches over which the Indians stretched skins.

Correct order: _____

2. (a) By the time of Hoover's death, the FBI had become the major national clearinghouse for crime information relayed by local and state law enforcement agencies and a model for law enforcement bodies everywhere. (b) Shortly afterwards, Hoover established a highly effective fingerprint and crime laboratory that was to become famous. (c) When he had assumed command of the Federal Bureau of Investigation in 1924, J. Edgar Hoover followed rigorous personal standards which carried over into his creation and administration of the Bureau. (d) Almost immediately, he required that agents hold either an accounting or law degree and that they be of impeccable personal morality. (e) Ultimately, the Bureau came to deal with crimes connected with civil rights in the 1960s, such as the case of the slaying of Mrs. Viola Liuzzo on a freedom march. (f) Eventually, the FBI became responsible for searching out and apprehending "public enemies" like John Dillinger and "Baby Face" Nelson, and for dealing in World War II with Nazi spies and saboteurs.

Correct order: _____

3. (a) Lemming's first role at the Pasadena Playhouse as Biff in *Death of a Salesman* made him known to theater fans throughout Southern California and earned him favorable reviews in trade papers. (b) In his eighth-grade play in Eau Claire, Wisconsin, Houston Lemming gave a performance of the tin woodsman in *The Wizard of Oz* that people still talk about. (c) Nearby Hollywood soon tapped his talent for the role of Sugar in Sam Sagonis's film *Dreamer with a Thousand Faces*, which was a success at the box office. (d) The senior plays at Eau Claire High School starred Houston Lemming in the lead roles of Shakespeare's *King Lear* and *Twelfth Night*. (e) Back on the West Coust, Houston received $25,000 per episode in his successful TV series *Ramsey*, in which he played a relaxed, but heavy-fisted, private detective. (f) During his hitch in the Army, Houston's performances as modern dramatic heroes and antiheroes gained him coverage in *Stars and Stripes*, the armed forces newspaper. (g) At the University of Wisconsin on the GI Bill, he gained campus fame for his portrayals of Lennie in the stage adapatation of John Steinbeck's *Of Mice and Men* and the gentlemen caller in Tennessee Williams's *The Glass Menagerie*. (h) The stage version of *Dreamer*—adapted from the film—played for fifty weeks to full houses at New York's Lincoln Center, with Houston drawing critical praise for his portrayal of Sugar. (i) From the beginning, Houston Lemming seemed destined for theatrical success.

Correct order: _____

EXERCISE 19   *The words in each of the following lists can be grouped into separate categories on the basis of association. After you have set up different categories, try to establish a logical order for the words within each of the categories. Use your own paper for this exercise.*

1. Tenderfoot, pupa, Exodus, Matthew, larva, First Class, egg, Genesis, adult, Mark, Star, John, Eagle, Luke, Life.
2. province, watt, neighborhood, Amazon, clarinet, volt, nation, piccolo, Nile, flute, Rhine, kilowatt, Misissippi, oboe, ampere, metropolis, bassoon, county, state.
3. salamander, centipede, centimeter, komodo dragon, spruce, sequoia, dinosaur, kilometer, coast redwood, beetle, ponderosa, iguana, meter, Douglas Fir, spider, millimeter, crocodile, millipede, decimeter, cedar, alligator.
4. excellence, affection, ineptitude, dislike, capability, tolerance, incompetence, love, mediocrity, passion.
5. ego, infancy, metamorphic, genocide, superego, senescence, igneous, id, patricide, adolescence, sedimentary, suicide, maturity, regicide.
6. mesomorph, Code of Hammurabi, James Earl Ray, pistil, Magna Carta, Lee Harvey Oswald, endomorph, Brutus, Bill of Rights, stamen, *Lex Romana*, anther, John Wilkes Booth, ectomorph.

EXERCISE 20   *This is an exercise to help you understand the use of repetition in a paragraph. Each of the underlined words is followed by certain words or phrases that refer back to it. Circle every word or phrase that refers to the underlined word, and draw a line connecting the word or phrase with its antecedent (the word it refers to).*

Whales—mammals of the scientific order Cetacea—are in all respects a widely varied species. (2) The *great blue* is the largest cetacean, an enormous creature which can consume 15,000 pounds of tiny crustaceans daily and which can gain up to 200 pounds of body weight a day in its formative years. (3) The blue, which grows to ninety feet in length at maturity, filters its food through baleen, a kind of strainer in its upper jaw. (4) The sperm whale, which reaches lengths of over fifty feet, is the largest "toothed" whale. (5) It eats fish and squid and can dive a mile, remaining submerged for as much as sixty minutes. (6) Perhaps the most unusual cetacean is the narwhal, which sports a single eight-foot spiraled tusk. (7) Narwhals, who seldom exceed fifteen feet in length, may be one of the sources of the unicorn legend. (8) The most aggressive of whales, the killer whale hunts in packs for fish, dolphins, other whales, and the seals which constitute the largest part of its diet. (9) This twenty-foot predator is a member of the dolphin family, and it shares the dolphin's formidable intelligence and great playfulness; it is also reasonably adaptable to captivity. (10) One of the most puzzling traits among cetaceans belongs to the small <u>pilot whale</u>, an animal that seldom exceeds seventeen feet in length. (11) Occasionally, pilots ram ashore in great numbers in a mass stranding. (12) Their tendency to destroy themselves is a phenomenon scientists cannot explain. (13) Whether it is baleen or toothed, reaches one hundred feet or fails to reach ten—the whale is a warm-blooded, air breather who bears live young and nourishes them with milk.

EXERCISE 21   *The following paragraph shows how coherence is achieved through the use of devices that link one idea to another. Moving from sentence to sentence, analyze the devices used for achieving coherence in this paragraph. Be prepared to discuss your findings in class.*

(1) Since the 12th Century, the powerful Percy family from Northumberland (the "North Country") has figured—for better or worse—in England's great national affairs. (2) In medieval times the Percys sometimes supported and sometimes harassed the Crown. (3) For example, Henry, 1st Lord Percy, fought the Scots for Edward II but later supported an insurrection against Edward, causing the Percys to be briefly disenfranchised. (4) In 1399 Henry Percy—Shakespeare's famous "Hotspur" in *Henry IV, Part I*—lost a revolt against the Crown, sacrificing in the process his estates (temporarily) and his head (permanently). (5) During the Renaissance Percys also made their presence felt in Court. (6) The 6th Earl, who was in love with Anne Boleyn, sadly yielded the lady to King Henry VIII, whose marriage with her produced the great Queen Elizabeth. (7) A half century later the 9th Earl of Northumberland was instrumental in bringing James I to England's throne, helping to avoid a foreign successor to the childless Queen Elizabeth. (8) In more modern times one of the Dukes of Northumberland served with distinction in the French Wars, another in the wars against the colonies, and a third in World War II. (9) Like his ancestors the present Duke occupies some impressive positions. (10) He is a Knight of the Garter, a Privy Councillor, and Lord Steward to the Crown. (11) In addition, he serves as a Member of Parliament and has headed a university. (12) When asked about some of his more politically reckless forebears—Hotspur, for example—the loyal 10th Duke answers with humorous understatement: "The power of government is such that to start a rebellion would be very difficult now."

ASSIGNMENT   *Write an essay or a long paragraph about how members of your family—or of a family you are personally acquainted with—have been historically instrumental in national, state, or local affairs. Or deal with a single family member who has thus distinguished himself/herself.*

Support

4

You probably recall our promise to discuss the subject of support in writing. Good writing must have concrete support, just as a bank must have sufficient capital. After all, facts, ideas, and illustrations are the writer's stock in trade, the coin he or she works with. Without authentic material to back it up, writing has no value. Poor writing is, in fact, a declaration of bankruptcy. The following student paragraph, despite certain unity and coherence, has no real content. There is no money in this bank:

> (1) Peter the Great of Russia was determined to change his country in positive ways. (2) He was a man of great size and ambition, so nothing about the Russian government of his time pleased him very much. (3) He was dissatisfied with just about everything he saw: he believed in self-improvement and national improvement. (4) This sometimes made him hard to live with. (5) He hated dishonesty, but what bothered him most was that people didn't want to do their fair share. (6) All in all, Peter left the impression that he was a very dissatisfied monarch.

It should be obvious to you that this paragraph needs content as much as Peter the Great thought Russia needed reform. All of the sentences are generalizations; not one of them even begins to support or develop the preceding sentence. Actually, any one of them would make a decent enough topic sentence for a paragraph of its own, but lumped together and passed off as a paragraph they put the student writer out of business.

To stay in business as a college student, you must take the trouble to get the facts. No one is interested in reading a series of generalizations; it's too hard for readers to relate them to their own lives, to their own situation in the world. Writing takes on interest for readers as it becomes *concrete.* Consider, for example, the fables of the Greek storyteller Aesop. Each tale serves to point up a moral or a bit of wisdom. You'll recall that in the story of the town mouse and the country mouse, two rodents travel to the home of the town mouse in search of a more luxurious way of life. But when they sit down to the leavings of a penthouse feast, they are frightened away by the dogs of the house. The tale ends with a message: better beans and bacon in peace than cakes and ale in fear.

The wisdom of Aesop's judgment about life is driven home by the *specifics,* by the details of the story itself. No one would be particularly happy to hear the moral repeated over and over again without the story. Your writing must combine specific facts with generalizations. For the present, you should try to concentrate more on detail than on generalization in your writing.

Specific Support

Perhaps the use of specific detail can best be illustrated by another paragraph about Peter's reforms.

> (1) From 1711 to 1725, Peter the Great devised and tried hard to implement the so-called Petrine reforms. (2) To replace the inefficient Boyar Council, he created a senate that could administer the government while he was absent on military campaigns. (3) In 1717 he instituted compulsory education for the younger sons of noble families who, when they reached age ten, were required to attend nonreligious schools. (4) Peter also revamped the rules of the growing civil service, considered at the time to be a very attractive and often lucrative occupation. (5) No more than a percentage of a family could serve; the major portion of the family men did compulsory military service. (6) He invented a position called Oberfiscal, an official who headed a department of men whose job it was to track down official corruption and bring it to trial. (7) Tzar Peter also raised capable commoners to positions of importance, making it possible for gifted men to acquire money and rise socially. (8) While many of his innovations ultimately failed, Peter was the first Russian ruler to make a serious try at transforming what was essentially a Medieval monarchy into a functioning Renaissance state.

You will probably find the above paragraph more convincing than the first one cited in this chapter. Undoubtedly, your increased interest results from the writer's use of specific content rather than generalizations. Notice the kind of facts that the writer uses. In sentence 1, for instance, compare the specific *Petrine reforms* with the vague "changes . . . in positive ways" in sentence 1 in the original paragraph. Note also that in the same sentence we are given the dates covering the time in which these reforms were launched. Sentence 2 in the revision gives us an example of a Petrine reform—a senate; and the writer exactly names the outmoded group it replaces, the *Boyar Council*. We learn in sentence 3 another date of a specific reform, *compulsory education*, as well as four other facts describing it. Sentence 4 specifies another reform. Sentences 5 and 6 delineate the reform with more facts, and give us another name *Oberfiscal* that specifically defines a new position in the new civil service. In sentence 7 we hear of an original and interesting Petrine innovation—the elevation of talented *commoners* to positions of *financial* and *social* power. And the concluding sentence, besides repeating the great reformer's name, sums up the paragraph by contrasting the names of two specific historical epochs, *Medieval* and *Renaissance*.

If you don't believe that it is the factual quality of the paragraph that improves writing, consider what happens if we eliminate a few specific details. Let's leave out *Petrine* and the dates in the first sentence and *Peter* and *first Russian ruler* and *Medieval* and *Renaissance* in the last sentence:

> Peter the Great devised and tried hard to implement some reforms. While many of his innovations ultimately failed, he made a serious attempt to change the government.

How vague and, hence, dull these sentences become when we omit some of the facts, names, and more specific details. And how much of the life has been drained from them. Names (like *Boyar Council* and *Oberfiscal*, *Medieval* and *Renaissance*) strategically placed, lend authentic detail and human interest to a piece of prose.

Perhaps at this point you think that most of what we're saying sounds all right in theory, but that professional writers probably don't make a federal case out of using specifics. For the hardened cynic, the following paragraph, from *Alistair Cooke's America*, might illustrate how an experienced professional *does* use details:

> (1) There was something else flourishing in the 1920s that was equally revolutionary to people who lived, say, a hundred miles from the nearest town. (2) I recall an advertising tycoon, Bruce Barton, saying in the late 1940s, when we were in a dither about the Russians: "What we ought to do is to send up a flight of a thousand B-29s and drop a million Sears, Roebuck catalogues all over Russia." (3) The mail-order catalogue arrived at the home of the farmer, cowboy, miner, and rancher, and they looked it over and realized that they had the world's biggest store in their mailbox. (4) The farmer could simply send off for all his equipment, from wagons and road scrapers down to his jeans. (5) His wife could riffle through sixty pages for clothes to buy and pick a cheap equivalent of what "smart" women were wearing in New York and Chicago. (6) And for ninety-five cents, her daughter could get the very hat that was worn by the "It Girl," Clara Bow, one of the first idols of the motion picture industry, which was beginning to serve a collateral function as the national store window for fashions of all sorts—bathing suits and hairdos and furniture and the cocktail habit and "companionate marriage" and many other fads and frivolities.

In the paragraph above, Alistair Cooke has satisfied the reader's curiosity about the power of mail-order buying to transform the habits—even the needs—of a whole society of consumers in the 1920s. In sentence 2 Cooke introduces a speaker by means of a quotation. Direction quotation renders "expert" opinion more convincing and is a dramatic means of imparting to a piece of writing the quality of the spoken word. In this instance, Bruce Barton's statement is a half-humorous belief that if mail-order purchasing were suddenly made available to average Russians, it would subvert their economic system and turn them into capitalists like us. In sentence 3 the writer introduces the particular consumer who will receive and use the catalogue. Sentence 4 speaks of some typical—but specific—purchases the farmer might make, and sentence 5 deals with his wife's choices from the catalogue. In sentence 6, the purchases made by the farmer's daughter are influenced by what was being worn in Hollywood by Clara Bow, the "It Girl" of the Roaring Twenties. Cooke's consistent use of such colorful and specific details keeps readers interested while it performs its major function—keeping readers informed.

Biographical writing also benefits by the inclusion of detail. The following paragraphs from William Prescott's *The Conquest of Mexico and the Conquest of Peru* deal with a crucial moment in Hernando Cortes's life when he was eighteen and still living at home, a continual worry and frustration to his highly respected parents.

> The youthful cavalier, however, hesitated whether to seek his fortunes under that victorious chief [Gonzalo de Cordoba, the "Great Captain," the most successful military commander of his time], or in the New World, where gold as well as glory was to be won, and where the very dangers had a mystery and romance in them inexpressibly fascinating to a youthful fancy. It was in this direction, accordingly, that the hot spirits of that day found a vent, especially from that part of the country where Cortes lived, the neighborhood of Seville and Cadiz, the focus of nautical enterprise. He decided on this latter course, and an opportunity offered itself in the splendid armament fitted out under Don Nicholas de Ovando, successor to Columbus. An unlucky accident defeated the purpose of Cortes.
>
> As he was scaling a high wall, one night, which gave him access to the apartment of a [married] lady with whom he was engaged in an intrigue, the stones gave way, and he was thrown down with much violence and buried under the ruins. A severe contusion, though attended with no other serious consequences, confined him to his bed till after the departure of the fleet.

In the first paragraph the *gold* and *glory* and *mystery* and *romance* and *hot spirits* perhaps foreshadow Cortes' brilliant and bloody conquest of Mexico. In the second paragraph the anecdote about his climb up the stone wall after the forbidden prize may suggest the courage, daring, and ruthlessness that never forsook him some years later in his famous march from the coast up to the valley of Mexico. Again, the writer takes the trouble to give us detail and an interesting anecdote fraught with meaning and portent of things to come.

Sources for Specifics

Where do you find these concrete, specific details that we've said provide substance in a piece of writing? Actually, there is more in the world to write about than most people think there is. For instance, metropolitan newspapers are a daily and inexhaustible depository of facts, magazine sections of Sunday newspapers being an especially rich source of factual materials for short, student papers. Some students, and teachers as well, have even been known to use advertisements as a source of detail. Books, especially nonfiction, are often filled with material that could be adaptable to your paragraphs. Among nonfiction sources, biography and autobiography are especially rich in specific detail and have the added advantage of dealing with human nature, always an interesting subject. Magazines are an excellent source of factual material: weekly and monthly journals of news and opinion, scientific and trade magazines, sports and various recreational periodicals—all of these go on year after year informing us about every subject (under the moon as well as under the sun), including the consequences of the daily acts of love and hate all over the world. And encyclopedias, both general and specific, are teeming with more facts and knowledge than most of us have ever dreamt existed.

Campus and public libraries abound with all of these publications. Use these libraries. Don't be afraid or too cocky to ask librarians for help. Most of them want to help you. Don't be discouraged by an occasional sour apple. We'll repeat it: believe us; most librarians want to help you. So ask for it.

But how do you properly use the details found in publications? Perhaps the best way to answer that question is to demonstrate step by step what one student did in constructing a paragraph out of facts found in the history *The Wheels of Commerce*, Volume 2, by the French historian Fernand Braudel. The following is an excerpt from this book, on which the student's paragraph is based.

> When it comes to beggars and vagrants, it is a very different story, and different pictures meet the eye: crowds, mobs, processions, sometimes mass emigrations, "along the country highways or the streets of the Town and Villages," by beggars "whom hunger and nakedness has driven from home" as Vauban notes.[162] There were sometimes brawls, always threats, occasionally fires, violent attacks and crimes. The towns dreaded these alarming visitors and drove them out as soon as they appeared on the horizon. But if shooed out at one door, they came in at another, in their vermin-ridden rags.[163]
>
> In the old days, the beggar who knocked at the rich man's door was re-

garded as a messenger from God, and might even be Christ in disguise. But such feelings of respect and compassion were disappearing. Idle, good for nothing and dangerous, was the verdict passed on the destitute by a society terrified by the rising tide of mendicancy.[164] Measures were repeatedly passed against begging in public, and against vagrancy which was before long classed as an offence. The vagrant was arrested, and "beaten over a wagon-end by the executioner,"[165] his head was shaved; he was branded with a red-hot iron, and warned that if caught again he would be hanged "without trial in any shape or form" or sent to the galleys where many vagrants did in fact end up.[166] From time to time, able-bodied beggars were rounded up and set to work, perhaps in specially created workshops; more often they were set to ditching, mending the town walls, or deported to the colonies.[167] In 1547, the English parliament decided that vagrants should simply be sent into slavery.[168] Two years later, the measure was revoked: parliament had been unable to agree who should receive these slaves and benefit from their labour, the state or private individuals. The idea was certainly in the air. Ogier Ghislain de Busbecq (1522–1572), the eminently civilized humanist who was Charles V's ambassador to Suleiman the Magnificent, thought that "if a just and mild form of slavery still existed, such as is prescribed by Roman law . . . there would not perhaps be need of so many gallows and gibbets to restrain those who possess nothing but their life and liberty and whose want drives them to crime of every kind."[169]

This was indeed the solution that prevailed in the seventeenth century— for what are imprisonment and forced labour but forms of slavery? Vagrants were put under lock and key everywhere, in the *alberghi de poveri* in Italy, the workhouses in England, in the *Discipline* in Geneva, in the *Zuchthauser* in Germany, and in the Parisian *maisons de force:* The Grand-Hôpital, built specially when the poor were "enclosed" in 1662, the Bastille, the Chateau of Vincennes, Saint-Lazare, Bicêtre, Charenton, the Madeleine and Sainte-Pelagie.[170] Sickness and death lent the authorities a helping hand. When the weather was severe and rations were short, mortality ran high in the workhouses, even when there was no epidemic. In Genoa in 1710, the workhouse had to be closed because there were so many corpses inside: the survivors were transferred to the Lazaretto, the quarantine-hospital where there were fortunately no infected patients. "The doctors say that these illnesses are merely the consequence of the want these poor people suffered last winter [i.e. the winter of 1709] and of the poor food they ate then."[171]

The student based the following paragraph on information taken from the above excerpt from Braudel's book. She titled her paragraph:

A FABLE FOR OUR TIME

The severity of the punishment of vagrants and beggars in Europe in the late Middle Ages suggests the fear and hatred the rest of the people felt for them. According to Fernand Braudel in *The Wheels of Commerce* in Volume 2, most beggary and vagrancy resulted from temporary and/or permanent unemployment. Although at first when men and women lost their jobs, others were sympathetic and patient toward them, as they grew poorer, hungrier, more burdensome, dirtier, and more desperate the others became more and more frightened of them, as for example as recorded in German towns in 1384, 1400, 1442, 1446, 1447. Reduced first to beggary, they would be forced out of their town or village into the countryside and highways cold, hungry and without shelter, where many perished. For example, according to an eye witness of the times, in 1662 there were corpses lying along most of the roads around the French town of Blois. Now the survivors became vagrants. Reaching a village or town, either the gates would be closed against them, as they were in the French town of Troyes in 1614, or a little help would be given them before they were turned away, or arrested, mistreated, and thrown into prison. Cruel indignities and corporal punishment inflicted on them attests to the dread they inspired in their more fortunate brothers and sisters who still had jobs and food and housing and fuel. Often they were beaten and flogged, heads shaved, convict marks seared into their flesh with branding irons, as found in records of the city of Paris in the years around 1550. Much of the time, without warning they were thrown into prison or shipped off to seaports to living deaths as galley slaves, records showing that in Paris five hundred poor people were sent off to be galley slaves in January, 1526. Back in 1547 England tried openly to enslave them. This plan failed only because parliament could not decide who was to profit off their slavery, private individuals or the English government. Then workhouses became a favorite solution: places of slavery, according to Braudel. But whether it was the workhouse where, typically in Genoa in 1710, there were so many dead of hunger, cold, and disease that there was no room for the living, who had to be transferred to a prison or prisons, the galleys, slavery in the colonies, about which we are told that Irish beggars in Paris in the early 1600s were sent to Canada and vagrants in Seville were sent to the Straits of Magellan—it was all inhumane. In Italy, France, England, Germany, Spain, all over Europe the beggars and the vagrants were either imprisoned or forced to live in conditions of such cold, hunger, filth, and general suffering and degradation, that they died in great numbers. Surely, the cruelty of this treatment reflects the terror inspired in the employed by others who for whatever reasons first became unemployed or unemployable, and then beggars, and then vagrants.

Perhaps you noticed that some of the most specific details (dates and places) in the student's paragraph were not in the excerpt on which she based her paragraph. Don't worry. The details were in the footnotes, 162–171, located in the back of Braudel's book. The student must be given credit for being a bit dissatisfied with the lack of specific detail in the text, and having the gumption to go to the back to find it, as indicated by the footnotes. Do you think this detailed factual material sharpened the paragraph's punch enough to justify the extra work and space?

At any rate, the student obviously was able to choose from the material and the excerpt the facts and details she wished to focus on to arrange it into a meaningful and coherent working order. Let's trace the method used to write this paragraph. The writer began by considering a number of possibilities for the main idea of the paragraph.

First possibility: Focusing on the subject of beggary and vagrancy in Europe in the late Middle Ages.

Decision: There is not enough information in the particular excerpt for this. The subject, also, is much too broad for a one-paragraph paper. The subject needs to be limited.

Second possibility: Focusing on the laws passed in an attempt to control beggary and vagrancy.

Decision: Such an approach could lead to a simple listing of such laws, which would be a dead end. However, it could turn into making a point about the nature of the laws, which would be narrower than the focus in the first possibility. Nevertheless, the focus still hasn't been defined clearly enough.

Third possibility: Focusing on the severity of the laws, with minor or subordinate attention paid to what this severity reveals about the attitudes of the rest of the population toward the beggars and vagrants.

Decision: This seems to be the most promising of the three approaches. The subject of the *severity* of the laws limits the topic sufficiently for the writer to *see* it and thus deal with it; and of course there is an abundance of material for developing this idea. Additionally, the subject of severity leads inevitably to the student's subordinate idea, which enables her to do more than merely paraphrase Braudel. It gives her a chance to say something *about* what Braudel says.

Now let's examine the steps taken in organizing the paragraph.

1. First the writer tries a tentative topic sentence:

   The severity of the punishment of beggars and vagrants in Europe in the late Middle Ages suggests the fear and hatred the rest of the people felt for them.

This sentence seems not too bad. The word *punishment* works better than *laws,* since laws are not always onerous unless they are enforced and/or harshly enforced.

2. The writer defines the key thought in the topic sentence as *severity of punishment.*

3. The rest of the paragraph must support and develop that idea.
   a. The outlawing of beggary and vagrancy, banishment from town and village, imprisonment, corporal punishment, enslavement, death because of hunger and exposure—all develop the subject of severity.

   b. Frequent reiteration of the feelings of the rest of the population as evidenced by the punishment keeps the minor idea alive, and this is necessary to give fullness to the paragraph.

c. The sheer weight of the amount of factual material devoted to the severity of the punishment gives that subject the emphasis that makes it dominate the entire paragraph.

4. Although the student-writer uses another writer's material, she works out a personal theory about the causal relationship between the majority feeling and the punishment, which is only implied by Braudel.

5. The student composed an appropiate ending, in which the final sentence essentially repeats the topic sentence, although in somewhat different words.

In the construction of this paragraph, the writer has first made a generalization from a group of specific details, and then has turned around and supported the generalization with the details *she has selected*. Note that the paragraph does not have the strict main clause unity we stressed so much before. Yet it does not sacrifice a singleness of purpose. By this point in the course, you may be ready to take the responsibility of maintaining unity without making each main clause agree with the controlling idea, so long as your paragraphs—like the one above—demonstrate a clear singleness of purpose. Perhaps you could also find your own approach to the facts you are interpreting. The student writer of "A Fable for Our Time" in her topic sentence suggests that the majority feeling is the cause and the punishment is the result. She proceeds to make the result her main idea and the cause the minor idea. Could you take essentially the same material and write a paragraph in which you make feelings (the cause) the main idea and the punishment (the effect) a minor idea?

Note 1: It has probably occurred to you, as you read both the excerpt and the student's paragraph, that some of the terms need definition: which ones? There will be more about this in Chapter 8.

Note 2: The student's rather jaunty title—while it is not quite accurate to call her piece a fable and while it just misses plagiarizing James Thurber's better known title *Fables for Our Times*—has its merits. First, as good titles always do, it adds something to the piece; second, the times she is writing about seem almost like another or *fabled* world to most of us; and third, in spite of the differences, the title suggests a basic similarity between that world and our world today that is almost inescapable. What is it?

Separating Fact from Opinion

By this time we have harped so much on the value of factual, specific support (as opposed to generalization) that we've surely become bores. Try to hang on as we attempt to make a final, clear distinction between a *fact* (sometimes called a *report*) and an *opinion* (sometimes called a *judgment* or *inference*). Check the differences between the following sets of facts and opinions:

Opinion	*Fact*
1. This morning the early sky was strikingly beautiful.	Waves of thick fog intermittently obscured the sun rising over the eastern ridge. Then the fog melted away, revealing a buttermilk sky.
2. Pasquale Ventimiglia is a savage fascist from Sicily, where he grew up in a typically violent Sicilian family.	Pasquale Ventimiglia is six feet two inches tall and weighs 205 pounds. He is one of Mussolini's bodyguards. On his off hours he plays the violin and sings Italian folk songs. He has been seen buying spumoni ice cream bars for kids in the neighborhood of his barracks. He was born and raised near Palermo, where his family has a small, but neat and productive, farm.
3. A steam locomotive is an accursed spawn of the devil.	A steam locomotive is a steel or iron vehicle with a built-in boiler and steam engine, which turns its drive wheels. It usually runs on steel rails, pulling cars with freight/passengers behind it. It gave rise to a story for children called *The Little Engine That Could.*
4. Watergate was a tragedy for the United States.	In June 1972, five men in the pay of the Committee for the Re-election of the President (Nixon) were caught breaking into the Democratic party's national headquarters in the Watergate Building in Washington, D.C. They were convicted of burglary and wiretapping. Their trials implicated among others, a number of men close to Nixon— John Mitchell, John Dean, J. S. Magruder, and Nixon's two closest advisors, H. R. Haldeman and John D. Erlichman. Finally, Nixon himself, disgraced and facing impeachment on sev-

Opinion	*Fact*

	eral counts, resigned on August 9, 1974. He was the only president of the United States ever to have resigned that office.
5. During wartime the United States pushes the panic button and restricts civil liberties.	In the Civil War, President Lincoln suspended the Writ of Habeas Corpus. During World War I, U.S. Supreme Court Justice Oliver Wendell Holmes denied first amendment rights to several writers of anti-draft pamphlets. In World War II, the Supreme Court allowed schools to compel children to salute the flag, even if this violated their religion. In 1942, the federal government evacuated about 12,000 Japanese-Americans from the West Coast and confined them in barracks hundreds of miles from their homes for two-and-a-half years.

As can be seen, facts are verifiable, objective statements based on measurement and observation. Any two of us looking at the dawn sky in example 1 would probably agree that the fog came and went in thick waves, that the sun when it appeared was bright and that finally there was a *buttermilk sky,* more or less. Regarding the beauty of the sky, however, there might be more opinions about it than that there were clouds in it, since standards of beauty tend to be a matter of individual taste, and may vary according to the way we feel at a particular moment. Your worrier, for example, might argue that the sky wasn't at all beautiful, rather, that it was a mixed-up sky, that the fog depressed him, made him apprehensive, afraid that it was going to be overcast all day, and that all those cream-colored clouds made him uneasy about the possibility of rain. Nevertheless, if you yourself liked the sky, then the opinion of its beauty is a valid inference to make based on the facts; and you have a perfect right to say so, as long as you don't insist that a person be broken on the wheel for disagreeing with you.

In example 2 there is nothing in the facts to justify the inferences (opinions) of *savage* and *violent,* or even *fascist;* and certainly it would be impossible to prove that the people in Sicily are ordinarily any more violent (or less) than the inhabitants of Milan, or Saskatchewan, or Lapland. Both opinions in examples 3 and 4 are valid inferences, either one as arguable as the other, depending on your point of view (where you are coming from). In example 5 the statement that the United States pushed the panic button is opinion, but the last part of the sentence—that the U.S. restricts civil liberties—is factual, for observer B would have to agree that civil rights are restricted; but he could disagree with the contention that in the process of restricting civil rights the country had pushed the panic button.

A good paragraph has a high ratio of facts to generalizations. A generalization is made in the topic sentence and repeated in the primary support, which is discussed in the next chapter. But the secondary support—the real substance of the paragraph—is long on fact and short on opinion. Consider the following paragraphs from *Alistair Cooke's America*. We will then try to make a distinction between fact and opinion. Remember, we are recommending that you extract the *facts* from a piece of prose, not that you borrow its opinions or imitate the style of the wording. We don't want you to be guilty of copying from a book or a magazine. However, facts are public property once they have been published.

(1) When Ford first sought financial backing, the very notion of farmers and shopgirls owning automobiles was so ridiculous that the House of Morgan told him to keep such daydreams to himself. (2) Ford rented a brick shed, managed to scrape together $28,000 in subscribed capital, and settled down to his daydream with a single-minded frenzy. (3) He sold seventeen hundred of his first model, a two-cylinder, eight-horsepower car with a chain drive, and in the next five years he tried out eight more models. (4) He was looking for a strong, cheap metal, which he finally found in an imported piece of vanadium steel, and in 1909 he used it on his first Model T.

(5) Ford, however barmy his politics or paranoid his later feelings about the Jews and trade unions, remains a giant of American history for one great reason: like Edison, he believed in supplying conveniences for the many rather than service for the few. (6) It was a belief that led straight to paper towels and cafeterias and supermarkets and motels. (7) Ford made his radical breakthrough by thinking first of the needs of hundreds of thousands of consumers. (8) His original labor policies made him the American god to employees, and his volcanic flow of productivity made him a terrible titan to his competitors. (9) In 1914 the national average wage was $2.40 a day. Ford paid a minimum of $5.00. (10) His first touring Model T cost $850. (11) By 1926, when he had quadrupled the average wage to nearly $10, the Model T sold for only $350 and had a self-starter. (12) It must have been a galling day for old J. P. Morgan when, as early as 1915, Ford drove his one millionth car off the assembly line. (13) By the end of the 1930s Ford had produced twenty-eight million cars.

(14) It is staggering to consider what the Model T was to lead to in both industry and folkways. (15) It certainly wove the first network of paved highways, subsequently the parkway, and then the freeway and the interstate. (16) Beginning in the early 1920s, people who had never taken a holiday beyond the nearest lake or mountain could now explore the South, New England, even the West, and in time the whole horizon of the United States. (17) Most of all, the Model T gave to the farmer and rancher, miles from anywhere, a new pair of legs.

Let's examine the factual content of this excerpt and distinguish it from opinion. The numbers below refer to the sentences in the quoted selection.

(1) . . . the very notion of farmers and shopgirls owning automobiles was so ridiculous that the House of Morgan told him to keep such daydreams to himself.

Opinion and generalization: This opinion can be well substantiated, however, by evidence from the financier J. P. Morgan's letters which show him as being disgruntled with Ford's egalitarian ideas about production.

(2) Ford rented a brick shed, . . . and settled down to his daydream with single-minded frenzy.

Fact: these facts are well documented in a great number of sources.
Opinion: Maybe Ford wasn't frenzied, but there's no doubt that he worked enormously hard to design a reliable automobile.

(3) He sold seventeen hundred of his first model. . . .

Fact: These details are well documented.

(4) He was looking for a strong, cheap metal, . . . and in 1909 he used it on his first Model T.

Fact: Ford, in his correspondence, indicates that he was seeking the ideal automotive alloy. First Model T: 1909.

(5) . . . however barmy his politics or paranoid his later feelings about the Jews and trade unions . . .

Opinion and generalization: Ford's quirkiness and political eccentricity are well-enough documented to need little substantiation.

. . . like Edison, he believed in supplying conveniences for the many rather than service for the few.

Fact: Ford's object—to provide personal transportation for the many—is also well known.

(6) It was a belief that led straight to paper towels and cafeterias and supermarkets and motels.

Opinion: This is the most daring speculation so far. But it's highly probable that Ford's organized production methods and division of labor inspired the organization of subsequent business enterprises and that the mass production of relatively inexpensive automobiles encouraged the output of other mass consumer goods and conveniences (i.e. paper towels).

(8) His original labor policies made him the American god . . .

Opinion and generalization: This is a highly "colored" judgment of Ford's industrial influence, but in the light of history it is probably no exaggeration.

(9 and 10) Ford paid a minimum of $5.00. His first touring Model T cost $850.

Facts: These statistics are documented.

(12) It must have been a galling day for J. P. Morgan. . . .

Opinion: Amusing supposition and speculation.

. . . as early as 1915, Ford drove his one millionth car off the assembly line.

Fact: By 1915 Ford had produced a million autos.

(13) By the end of the 1930s Ford had produced twenty-eight million cars.

Fact.

You'll quickly see that the third paragraph contains the greatest concentration of opinion—or, at least, of facts that cannot readily be substantiated by statistics. Perhaps in 1920 many Americans had never taken a holiday beyond the nearest lake or mountain. Perhaps the Model T had help from other makes of automobiles in inspiring the paved highway and finally the interstate, but it is true that the Model T was strongly *contributory* to the development of modern American roads. If one grants the preceding point, then Cooke's final metaphor—the car as new legs—probably holds true too.

It is important to realize that Alistair Cooke has *earned* the right to generalize and speculate by first offering the reader a vivid body of substantiating evidence to back the claims of the essay about the vast influence of Ford's production theories. All these factual details (or details like them) could also be used by you if you were to write a paragraph about the power that a single, timely commodity sometimes exercises over the habits and customs of an entire society.

Let's review the ways for establishing concreteness and factuality in a piece of writing. These methods include the use of the following:

1. The names of persons (*J. P. Morgan, Edison*) and their involvement in the concerns the article is dealing with.
2. The names of institutions *(the House of Morgan)* and their relation to the concerns of the article.
3. Quotations—direct or indirect—and the identification of the people who made them. (Cooke uses a quotation in the paragraph on the influence of the Sears catalogue, page 67.)
4. Sections or regions of the country *(South, New England, the West)*. Geographic locations are good concrete references.
5. Dates (*1914, 1920s*) that establish an historical point of reference and evoke an era.
6. Numbers that give the reader a concrete basis upon which to make comparisons. (How many numbers—amounts, figures, estimates—does Cooke use in this three-paragraph excerpt?)
7. The narration of events that took place.

Avoiding Plagiarism

A constant danger in using facts from any source is that you will plagiarize, which means copying verbatim or even paraphrasing too closely what is found in an original source. To avoid plagiarism, try following these practical suggestions:

1. If you use a fact or facts from a source, name the source in your paragraph (or in a footnote if you are writing a heavily documented paper).
2. More important, reword the factual statement in your own vocabulary. Do not lift the statement in its exact wording from its source.
3. Avoid using the same descriptive words (verbs, as well as adjectives and adverbs) that are found in the original text. Look out for emotionally loaded words, such as *scrambled, thrust, blasted, cheated, hostile, brutal, exterminated, sterile, violent, honest,* and so on.
4. Avoid restating the writer's opinions. Develop your own opinions based on the facts.
5. If you do use the writer's opinions, be sure to distinguish clearly between the writer's opinions and your own, and between facts and opinions in your source; credit the writer's opinions in a note.

The following passage has been excerpted from George Orwell's essay "Reflections on Gandhi." After you have studied the excerpt and the student paragraph that follows it, you will have a better understanding of what constitutes plagiarism and should be able to avoid it in your own writing.

However, Gandhi's pacifism can be separated to some extent from his other teachings. Its motive was religious, but he claimed also for it that it was a definite technique, a method, capable of producing desired political results. Gandhi's attitude was not that of most Western pacifists. *Satyagraha*, first evolved in South Africa, was a sort of non-violent warfare, a way of defeating the enemy without hurting him and without feeling or arousing hatred. It entailed such things as civil disobedience, strikes, lying down in front of railway trains, enduring police charges without running away and without hitting back, and the like. Gandhi objected to "passive resistance" as a translation of *Satyagraha:* in Gujarati, it seems, the word means "firmness in the truth." In his early days Gandhi served as a stretcher-bearer on the British side in the Boer War, and he was prepared to do the same again in the war of 1914–18. Even after he had completely abjured violence he was honest enough to see that in war it is usually necessary to take sides. He did not—indeed, since his whole political life centered around a struggle for national independence, he could not—take the sterile and dishonest line of pretending that in every war both sides are exactly the same and it makes no difference who wins. Nor did he, like most Western pacifists, specialize in avoiding awkward questions. In relation to the late war, one question that every pacifist had a clear obligation to answer was: "What about the Jews? Are you prepared to see them exterminated? If not, how do you propose to save them without resorting to war?" I must say that I have never heard, from any Western pacifist, an honest answer to this question, though I have heard plenty of evasions, usually of the "you're another" type. But it so happens that Gandhi was asked a somewhat similar question in 1938 and that his answer is on record in Mr. Louis Fischer's *Gandhi and Stalin.* According to Mr. Fischer, Gandhi's view was that the German Jews ought to commit collective suicide, which "would have aroused the world and the people of Germany to Hitler's violence." After the war he justified himself: the Jews had been killed anyway, and might as well have died significantly. One has the impression that this attitude staggered even so warm an admirer as Mr. Fischer, but Gandhi was merely being honest. If you are not prepared to take life, you must often be prepared for lives to be lost in some other way. When, in 1942, he urged non-violent resistance against a Japanese invasion, he was ready to admit that it might cost several million deaths.

Now let us consider a student's paragraph based on George Orwell's paragraph:

(1) Although Gandhi's pacifism resembles that of many Westerners, it differs from it in several very important ways. (2) Like many Westerners' pacifism, its motive was religious, and it was used as a means of achieving good political results. (3) But Gandhi believed in *Satyagraha,* a sort of nonviolent

warfare, which "involved civil destruction, strikes, getting in the way of railroad trains, sustaining police charges without running or striking back." (4) In the Boer War Gandhi was a stretcher-bearer on the side of the English and was ready to do the same again for the British in the First World War, and even after he came out against violence, he was honest enough to see that in war it is usually necessary to take sides. (5) He did not take the sterile and dishonest line of believing that all wars are the same and that it doesn't make any difference who wins. (6) Also, unlike most Western pacifists, he never forgot that under some forms of oppression and tyranny great numbers of people might be killed even if they did not resist—witness annihilation of the Jews during the Second World War. (7) According to Louis Fischer, Gandhi said that the German Jews should have committed collective suicide. (8) This would have called the world's attention to their troubles, and it didn't make any real difference because they were all killed anyway. (9) This way, at least, their deaths would have had some significance. (10) In 1942, he urged nonviolent resistance against the Japanese invasion of India. (11) He said it might cost several million deaths. (12) So you can see how Gandhi's pacifism is different from most Westerners'.

To examine briefly for plagiarism: The underlined words in sentences 1, 2, 3, 4, 5, 7, 8, 10, and 11 are Orwell's, not the student's, and the student has used them without giving Orwell credit through the use of quotation marks. In sentence 3 the quotation is not verbatim and hence inaccurate. Remember, all quotations must be exactly the same as they were in the source. In sentence 4 the student presents Orwell's opinions as if they were the student's own—they might well be, but Orwell stated them first, and he must be given credit for them. This is easy to do: Use "According to Orwell," "Orwell says," "Orwell believes," or something of that sort, and you are covered. Without doing that, you are plagiarizing another person's thoughts. In addition, sentence 4 contains plagiarized words and structures. In sentence 5 the structure and, again, many of the words are Orwell's, but no credit is accorded him. Complete the analysis of the paragraph yourself. Study each sentence separately and see how many examples of plagiarism you can find and define.

The principal origin of the plagiarism in the student paragraph is in the writer's failure to give us a personal reaction to Orwell's work. The writer is merely attempting to paraphrase the passage. Because the student was writing primarily from Orwell's page, Orwell's thoughts, words, and structures automatically came tumbling out onto the student's page; there is no original thinking from the student. The following paragraph is the final version, in which the student made an effort to give personal opinions of the facts and ideas rather than Orwell's.

(1) According to Orwell, Gandhi's pacifism was quite different from the pacifism of most Westerners. (2) A follower of *Satyagraha*, the Indian name for Gandhi's form of pacifism, does take sides. (3) He does not use physical violence, but he resists aggression in various other ways. (4) He takes the side of the people he agrees with, and from that position he faces the enemy.

(5) He deliberately gets in their way; he says "no" whenever he can. (6) He will choose to starve or maybe even be shot down rather than submit, and in his own way he will give the enemy plenty of trouble at the time. (7) To me this is more courageous and honest, if you are a pacifist, than just saying, "all quarrels and wars are lousy and, therefore, I won't take sides." (8) But I think Gandhi realized that in some cases many people might die if they practiced nonviolent resistance. (9) He said, for example, that the German Jews should have "committed collective suicide" as a form of protest. (10) Well, as terrible as that sounds, I agree that it would have had more meaning than not resisting at all and yet dying anyway. (11) Although I personally sympathize with most American pacifists, I would agree with both Orwell and Gandhi that any pacifist who says that all wars and all sides are equally evil has not thought very deeply about his pacifism.

Whatever the shortcomings of this paragraph, it is honest, and it is the result of some thinking on the student's part—the student has not simply repeated Orwell's ideas, words, and grammatical constructs. This paragraph is acceptable, because it is free of plagiarism, whereas the one before it is not. Anyone who makes use of outside sources to obtain information for writing must make a constant effort to avoid plagiarism. It isn't wrong to rely on what you read. You have every right to increase your knowledge by consulting outside sources for information, but in using that material in your writing, you must find your own words, style, and thoughts.

SUMMARY

1. Good writing is a combination of opinion and fact, but, practically speaking, more fact than opinion is desirable in most student writing.
2. Topic sentences convey an opinion that most of the remaining sentences support factually.
3. Specifics (concrete items) include such things as numbers, names, titles of works, geographic locations, statistics, quotations, and the narration of events that took place.
4. Useful sources of specific details include newspapers, biographical and nonfictional works, news magazines, textbooks, and one's own observations.
5. Fact deals with what actually occurred or exists; opinion makes a judgment concerning that actual occurrence or state of being.
6. Cite your source somewhere in your paragraph.
7. Above all, any material that you use must be expressed *in your own words* and not in the words of a professional writer. Base your own opinions on the facts. Come to your own conclusions regarding the facts.

Facts are the *substance* of a piece of writing—the marks of its authenticity. You can't write convincingly unless you have something to write about. Maybe even old Aesop would agree with us when we conclude with a moral of our own:

You can't make chicken salad out of feathers.

EXERCISE 22 *In the blank preceding each of the following statements, write F if the statement is fact or O if it is an opinion.*

_____ 1. Americans are the most freedom-loving people in the world.

_____ 2. The legal basis for the civil rights of Americans is in the first ten amendments to the U.S. Constitution.

_____ 3. In 1934 in California it was against state law for Filipinos and "white" persons to marry.

_____ 4. This was a bad law.

_____ 5. This was a good law.

_____ 6. This law violated the U.S. Constitution.

_____ 7. Near Agra in northern India a man named Goonga charges onlookers five rupees in return for performing a 170-foot dive into a reservoir 40 feet deep that is always at least half full of water.

_____ 8. The people of India can do many things that Occidentals can't because the Indians have more religious faith.

_____ 9. William Least Heat Moon, part American Indian, wrote a book titled *Blue Highways*.

_____ 10. The American teacher and writer Robert Penn Warren called the book a "masterpiece."

_____ 11. *Blue Highways* is the finest piece of writing produced in America in 1983.

_____ 12. Television is subverting the mental and moral education of American children.

_____ 13. We should pass legislation restricting the growth of industries that produce poisonous waste products.

_____ 14. High concentrations of smog are unhealthful.

_____ 15. Smog has ruined the Los Angeles area.

_____ 16. Graciela Cassilas is the International Women's Boxing Association bantamweight champion. She is five feet four inches tall and weighs 116 pounds.

_____ 17. Three thousand dollars is the most money that Ms. Cassilas has ever been paid for a fight.

_____ 18. She doesn't deserve to make more money because male audiences get more entertainment out of watching female mud wrestlers.

_____ 19. The Canadian-American, Henri (Frenchy) LaMothe, at the age of seventy dove from a height of forty feet into a kid's play pool of water only twelve inches deep, and suffered no injuries.

_____ 20. Only faith—in himself, if not in religion—could enable a man to do this.

EXERCISE 23 *Extract the facts from each of the following sentences and create your own sentence from these facts. First, cross out any word or phrase that is not factual. You may substitute or add a neutral word(s) or phrase, as needed, to make sense out of what remains.*

Example:

Original: At 3:30 P.M., August 17, 1983, Maude Whitehead, the notorious left-winger on the Board of Supervisors, delivered her heavily biased report to the Mayor's Commission on Poverty in a fake-genteel, simpering manner.

Revision: At 3:30 P.M., August 17, 1983, Maude Whitehead, liberal member of the Board of Supervisors, delivered her report to the Mayor's Commission on Poverty.

1. A lot of weird people like Ephraim Potlach, Johanna Kerensky, Porfirio Rubirosa, Joe Bommarito, Anders Anderson, F. Fitzpatrick (Chuckie) Montgomery, and Joan Smith, each carrying a little plastic carton of tasteless yogurt, showed up at the pinko demonstrators' picnic.
2. Most of the people in favor of the Commie-controlled, Freeze-the-Bomb Movement are sincere bleeding hearts who are simply afraid to fight.
3. For thirty minutes, the defense attorney grilled J.D. Jackson, beefy, florid Muskaloosa County sheriff, whose cornpone, surface manner hides the brutality that allegedly caused county jail prisoners to scream about conditions to Governor Arkley J. Wright last May.
4. In the smoke-filled, beery air of a back room in a sleazy, South Third Street saloon, under the steely gaze of "Quiet Guy" Manuel Quintero, Soapy Callahan's luck ran out.
5. Colonel Phillip da Vinci, boss of America's ZYX missile program, impeccably dressed, scholarly, and exquisitely mannered, parried Congressman Ross Hart's sledgehammer-like questions with a civilized urbanity matched only by the incisive and convincing substance of his arguments.
6. Beefy Senator Wolfgang von Pufendorf described the Reagan administration's foreign policy as consisting of "the iron fist of threatened force inside the velvet glove of diplomacy."
7. In his usual rude and uncivil manner, Congressman Ross Hart, commenting on the fat, little senator's statement, said, "Baloney, there ain't any velvet glove."
8. When the naive and unrealistic Save-the-Whales people had their con-

frontation with the Russians in July, 1983, American rednecks and fascist hardhats couldn't decide which ones to make fun of.

EXERCISE 24   *In the following short essay, from,* Journal of a War, *the author, Donald Pearce, sketches the character of a Belgian woman he met while serving in the Canadian Army in World War II. Develop your own paragraph from the facts and observations in the essay. Before you begin to write, answer the questions that follow the article. Be sure to use your own words in your writing.*

ROSALIE

Life [the author's, not the peasants] among the peasants of Belgium has been extremely pleasant; in fact, delightful. The platoon is quartered in a bar, but I—thank God—am in a farmhouse, where I occupy the spare bedroom and can observe what goes on inside this beehive. The day begins at 4:30 A.M. At that time I can hear Rosalie, the fifty-year-old woman who runs this little farm, padding to and fro in soft slippers doing I know not what to the stove, the dishes, the kitchen, and the pantry. By the time I get up, a couple of hours later, the cows have been attended to, breakfast prepared, the washing hung out, apples peeled, eggs collected, and other unseen tasks performed. Rosalie waves me to the kitchen table; and, though the gruel is curiously sour, I must eat, for she has made it especially for me and has filled it full of her best grains and buttermilk. She nods, smacks her lips, smiles her head, in vicarious delight, with every spoonful I take. I smile and grunt right back, and lately I have meant it for the flavor of the stuff begins to grow on you.

I've watched Rosalie for days now, and have not once seen her idle. Her day is geared to the minute hand of the kitchen clock, and neither she nor it ever stops. Her whole life must have been spent in continuous activity, or rather service, and it has bent her over. Inactivity is obviously immoral to her. If there is no big task to hand, like kneading huge quantities of dough on her knees, by the stove, she polishes the stove-lifter, waxes the table top, scrubs the doorstep, shines the windows. She is constantly cleaning. Yet she hasn't the faintest idea of real sanitation. A primitive cleanliness is all that she understands. She scrubs the floor each day with boiling water, but the hands that have wrung out the mop plunge themselves tirelessly and deep into the heavy dough. She scalds the dishes and then dries them with a dirty cloth. She cleans the forks with a far-from-immaculate apron. She wears herself out. She has done so for at least forty years, and now she can no longer walk upright, but moves bent over, hustling here and there from one corner of the room to another, led by a momentary fixed idea rather than a plan of work. The salt is at the opposite end of the kitchen from the pepper, the butter from the milk, but she always returns them to these disparate places in the scuttling darkness of her low-beamed kitchen.

Her brother Raymond, who is a widower, is about Rosalie's age. He sits by the stove most of the day, warming his back and soaking his lame foot in water. He does little work, and probably never has; his foot is only sprained from a fall. Work has never bent him over, or any of the other men I see in this district. They are like dwindled feudal lords, and the women are their uncomplaining serfs. Girls of fourteen do hard barnyard work, or labor in the fields all day long. They will all be Rosalies at last, you can see it coming. They carry pails of milk or water suspended at their sides from yokes that fit over their shoulder, haul baskets of potatoes, and only stop pulling up acres of mangels for half an hour for lunch. Boys of the same age work much less, ride bicycles most of the time, and in the evenings talk to the soldiers in the taverns.

Rosalie is strictly religious. Her day begins with matins and closes with an evening prayer. She prays silently and like a statue before and after each meal. On all the walls of the rooms she has pinned up religious pictures which she has cut from calendars or magazines. Here and there are sacred mottoes and phrases, done in *petit-point* and set in little frames above doorways. Mantelpieces are laden with metal crucifixes and silver figures of saints and angels in a variety of attitudes. By candlelight, these effigies gleam softly along the walls like peering eyes. Rosalie lifts them, straining upwards with apparent tenderness, and dusts off the spots on which they stand, and puts them softly back. There are two before which she blesses herself.

At night, perhaps ten of the men from the platoon gather in the kitchen. We sit around a big table, the top of which is never completely dry because Rosalie scrubs it three times every day, and in the glow of the single candle we raise a great deal of noise and laughter, eat huge helpings of creamed potatoes, and gulp down cognac. In the background, quite in the shadows, four or five visitors sit smoking their pipes beside the stove, and watch our party. Rosalie peels a peck or more of potatoes while we are there, never looking down as she works and never breaking a single peel; they lie in a great curling pile at her feet, like a pile of carpenter's shavings. We get noisier and noisier, and Rosalie peels faster and faster, till her fingers fairly flicker and her hair comes loose in wisps about her forehead. We stand beside the stove in a large dim group, and everybody tries to talk Flemish to the visitors. They offer us cigars, we give them cigarettes, and the place so fills with smoke that there is a bright halo around the candle. When we fail to understand them, which is usually, they shout at us as if we were deaf, poking their whiskered faces near our ears.

We sing a song or two, and prepare to leave. Rosalie sees each one out, guiding them through the cluster of wooden shoes near the door; they look like a fleet of little tied-up gondolas. Then the visitors leave, indicating to me with their hands beside their cheeks that they are going to go to bed. Rosalie makes me some hot milk, washes the dishes in a nearly dark corner, and starts to mix some applesauce, at which she can still be heard working long after I have gone to bed. I read a French newspaper by candlelight and listen to stray aircraft carrying bombs or supplies to the front. It is a deep and comfortable bed, and I never wake up all night.

1. List five or more adjectives that you think best describe Rosalie's character.

2. Choose the *one* adjective or phrase that you think has the best possibility for development with the facts found in the article and define that key word.

3. Make that word or phrase the controlling idea in one of the following topic sentences:

 a. At the time of World War II there lived in Belgium Rosalie, a peasant woman, in whom _____ was the outstanding characteristic.

 b. Although the men and the boys acted like lords and masters, Rosalie's _____ seemed to dominate life on the farm.

4. Choosing one of these topic sentences, make a list of specifics from the essay that support your controlling idea in the way you have used it in your topic sentence.

TS: _____

 I. _____

   A. _____

   B. _____

 II. _____

   A. _____

   B. _____

5. Using your fact sheet or outline, write a unified, coherent, factually supported paragraph of at least 130 words.

EXERCISE 25   *The following article taken from the* Encyclopaedia Britannica *is by Victor M. Cassidy. Read it and complete the exercises that follow it.*

SHIRLEY MULDOWNEY

"It is strange to see a woman drive one of these cars competitively . . . I beat the fellows, I don't just sandbag. I'm in there to win, not just because I'm a woman." So says Shirley ("Cha Cha") Muldowney, the only woman in the world who is professionally licensed to drive a Top Fuel dragster. This machine covers a quarter-mile track in less than six seconds, attaining a final speed of about 250 m.p.h. (400 km/h). The 2,500-hp engine, which is pushed to its performance limit with extreme speed, may explode or catch fire. If this happens, and it has happened more than once to Muldowney, large quantities of burning nitromethane fuel fly everywhere. The very rapid acceleration of a dragster puts the driver's body under stresses that are two or three times the force of gravity. According to Muldowney, driving under such conditions is like "controlling a runaway roller coaster."

 Muldowney, who was about 40 in 1981, began to race cars at the age of 14 in the streets of Schenectady, New York. When she was 16 she dropped out of school to marry Jack Muldowney, an auto mechanic. Together they raced stock cars and dragsters. She drove, and he repaired the engines. The marriage ended after 15 years, and Shirley Muldowney continued racing on her own. In 1981 her crew included her grown son John.

Not all male drivers welcomed Muldowney into their ranks, and she has some unpleasant memories of hostile treatment while she was on her way up. Even when she won the national Top Fuel dragster championship in 1977, the previous titleholder declared afterward that he was "not above punching her out." In spite of this Muldowney refuses to be angry. "They're all my friends now," she says. "Now they don't hate me."

1. The facts/details in the first paragraph talk mainly about _____
_____ .

The details in the second paragraph are mainly biographical, that is, they directly tell us something about Shirley Muldowney's life.
The details in the third paragraph are mainly about _____ .
2. What does each of the three paragraphs, even if only indirectly, tell us about Ms. Muldowney?
3. Consider the following type of topic sentence as a beginning:

In attaining (achieving or accomplishing) _____ _____
_____ _____ , Shirley Muldowney has to _____
_____ _____ _____ .

The controlling idea should be in the main clause, which begins with "Shirley Muldowney."
4. With this type of topic sentence, or a different one of your own choosing, write a paragraph of at least 300 words based on the Cassidy article.

EXERCISE 26   *Read the following paragraph; then complete the assignment based on it.*

(1) The messages contained in Harley-Davidson advertising brochures promise escape or play on the prospective buyer's ego by suggesting that he can greatly enhance his image simply by owning a Harley-Davidson motorcycle. (2) Harley's ad for the 65cc Leggero, for example, suggests that its machine is "Big enough and strong enough to carry you wherever the spirit moves you," a clear salute to the freedom and largeness of soul of the rider. (3) Moreover, the Leggero is, according to the manufacturer, "Your ticket out of a world you never made," an appeal that the young and disenchanted might respond to. (4) The message in Harley's ad for their larger Rapido lives up to the name of the machine. (5) "Savage aggressiveness in the open country" is what the Rapido features, perhaps for the genuinely aggressive or for those who can safely pretend they are while aboard a Rapido. (6) Harley's ad for their two Sportster 1,000 models promises therapy along with transportation in "Machines that straighten it all out . . . on the street, the strip or in your mind." (7) Harley's big bike, the 1,200cc Electra Glide is "a machine great enough to meet the expectations of a special kind of man." (8) Of course, what is implied is that the reader is that "special kind of man." (9) After all,

who wouldn't enjoy the distinctiveness conferred on him merely by owning the Electra Glide? (10) Judging from the ads, the cost of any of these vehicles is an investment in personal uniqueness, manliness, and aggressive individuality.

The writer of this paragraph is responding to the message of the Harley brochures quite differently from the way the company probably hoped he would. He's making a judgment about the nature of the appeal projected by the ads, seeing that appeal as based on a kind of propaganda. This propaganda promises the buyer something *more* than simply a means of transportation: increased sexuality, personal charisma, aggressiveness, luxury, therapy.

Using magazines, newspapers, advertising brochures, TV ads, or a combination of any or all of these, write a paragraph analyzing the appeals used by advertisements for a certain kind of product. Pay special attention to the *name* of the product: "Toronado," "Barracuda," "Rapido." Below are some possibilities:

1. Automobiles
2. Pickup trucks
3. Household furnishings
4. Cosmetics
5. Pleasure boats
6. Sports equipment
7. Clothing

EXERCISE 27 *Using the same material the student used in her "A Fable For Our Time," including the footnoted material not appearing in the excerpt, write a paragraph in which your topic sentence's controlling idea is the attitude of the employed part of the population toward the beggars and the vagrants. In such a paragraph the cause (the people's attitude) becomes the main idea, while the effect (the severity of the punishment) becomes the minor or subordinate idea.*

EXERCISE 28 *Study the following excerpt from the essay on the Brooklyn Bridge, titled "The Great Bridge and the American Imagination," by David McCullough.*

Once, while going through the great collection of Roebling papers and family memorabilia that had been locked away for years in a storage closet in the old library at Renssalaer Polytechnic Institute in Troy, N.Y., I found among a bundle of letters one of the original invitations engraved by Tiffany for the opening ceremonies [the opening of the Brooklyn Bridge May 24, 1883]; I had an odd urge to dash off a note of acceptance.

But what was the celebration all about? Why such a fuss over the Brooklyn Bridge, then and now? Soon it will be 100 years old, but nothing we've ever built holds quite the same place in our lives. In a sense, the celebration has never stopped.

We have written songs about it, photographed it, etched it on glass, embroidered it on pillows.

It has been sketched and painted as has no other structure and often with powerful results. (Contemporary artists comment on the bridge on page 80.) A collection of paintings and lithographs of the Brooklyn Bridge currently exhibited at the Brooklyn Museum, as part of the centennial celebration, includes the work of George Bellows, Childe Hassam, Louis Guglielmi, Georgia O'Keefe, Joseph Pennell and Joseph Stella, some of whom, like Stella, have painted it several times.

It figures repeatedly in our literature—in novels by John Dos Passos and Thomas Wolfe, poems by Hart Crane and Marianne Moore, an essay on New York by Henry James. It is the setting for the Maxwell Anderson play "Winterset," and it is the bridge in Arthur Miller's *A View from the Bridge*, which is again on Broadway this year.

It shows up at every level of our culture. It has been taken light-heartedly ("All that trouble just to get to Brooklyn!" was an old vaudeville appraisal) and with a seriousness sometimes verging on the mystical—Hart Crane's epic poem "The Bridge" being a supreme example. For Crane, the bridge was a "Tall Vision-of-the-Voyage," the "silver-paced" redeeming symbol at the heart of American history.

It has been regarded as a major American work of art from the time it was built. The first serious review of an American structure to appear in a popular American journal was a rave in *Harper's Weekly* by a man named Montgomery Schuyler the week of the grand opening. In the time since, the critic Lewis Mumford has hailed it as a "joy and inspiration." At Yale, for thirty-six years now, Vincent Scully's brilliant lecture on the bridge—part of his course on modern architecture—has been a high point in undergraduate life. To Scully, the bridge is an "incomparable" symbol of the United States: "It is the most majestic embodiment of the American experience of the road—of leaping free." The architect Philip Johnson has said that the bridge and Central Park are his favorite works of architecture in New York.

It has also had a surpassing movie career. In 1899, Thomas Edison made it the subject of one of his earliest experiments in motion pictures. It can be seen in *Tarzan's New York Adventure* and Laurel and Hardy's *Way Out West*. More recently, it has made prominent appearances in *Annie Hall* and *Sophie's Choice*. A documentary on the bridge by Ken Burns—which was made for public television and which will be shown the night of May 25—was a nominee for an Academy Award last year.

The only other New York icons with a screen presence anything like that of the Brooklyn Bridge are the Empire State Building and the Statue of Liberty, and while the Empire State Building's memorable encounter with King Kong remains in a class by itself, there is really no question as to which of these monuments holds first place.

Frank Sinatra sang about the Brooklyn Bridge; Bugs Bunny "sold" it. Its image has been used to peddle everything from sewing machines and cigarettes to Coca-Cola, Kentucky Fried Chicken, fur coats and high-style cowboy boots. It has appeared on postcards, Christmas cards, record jackets.

It's been printed, painted, or stamped on paperweights, ashtrays, T-shirts, silver spoons. It has done its turn as calendar art, as the symbol for a television channel, as the label for Dr. Brown's Cel-Ray soda.

Nor is the bridge's appeal limited to this country. It is, for example, among the few American works mentioned in "Civilization," the series of filmed lectures by the eminent British art critic Kenneth Clark. Brooklyn Bridge chewing gum happens to be a big seller in Italy. In the Netherlands, a man named Ed Schilders puts out The Brooklyn Bridge Bulletin, a small paper devoted exclusively to the subject. "Loving the Brooklyn Bridge is a part of being human," wrote one of the bulletin's readers in a recent letters-to-the-editor column.

Part of the explanation has to do with the bridge's place in the history of New York and its prominence as a symbol of old-fashioned 19th century American progress. It was built by a generation that believed wholeheartedly in a shining American future with New York as its vital center—the generation that also built St. Patrick's Cathedral, the American Museum of Natural History, Central Park and the Metropolitan Museum of Art.

To John A. Roebling, who died horribly a few months before construction of the bridge began, there was never a question about the importance of the bridge. In his initial formal proposal of 1867, he declared that the bridge would not only rank as the greatest ever built, and the greatest work of civil engineering in the land, and a great work of art, it would also stand the test of time. It would endure as a monument to the people who made it possible.

And so it has, bridging the great divide between our time and theirs as much as it bridges the East River.

It rises out of an age so very different and distant from our own, and yet there it is. We are more accustomed to the "real past" behind glass in a museum case, or gussied up as it is in Williamsburg. But this is the genuine article. And it works, still, when so much else doesn't.

The late 19th century is part of our history best remembered for its low politics and the extravagances of the new rich. Yet out of it rises this most magnificent triumph of perseverance and belief in excellence. Only a society of enormous confidence and vitality could have produced such a monument. Today, at a time of diminished expectations and growing national self-doubt, the bridge is a particularly appropriate symbol of affirmation—that America has dared to be great and still can.

Up to the last four paragraphs this excerpt is exceptionally rich in detail. Start at the beginning of the passage and go through it making a brief list of the details. Notice that most of these details are honors of a sort, in a sense prizes, that the Brooklyn Bridge has won or that have been bestowed on her by admiring, observant and thoughtful, or even by opportunistic people. Scan through your list and on another piece of paper classify them under five or six, or seven different headings. You might use such categories as ARTISTIC, LITERARY, COMMERCIAL, and so on. Then compose a sentence about each of these headings in its relation to the Brooklyn Bridge and use one or two or a few of your details to illustrate and fill out your sentence.

Example: Undoubtedly, fortunes have been made off the bridge; it has been used decoratively on postcards, Christmas cards, and calendars, or as a symbol or motif in such a product as *"Brooklyn Bridge Chewing Gum,"* which is highly successful in Italy.

Next study these sentences—you should have at least six of them—and write another sentence summarizing or generalizing about them, in which you clearly focus on one distinctly expressed idea about them all. Then, using this last sentence as your topic sentence, with its main idea as your controlling idea, set it at the head of a piece of paper and using your other six or so sentences to develop your topic sentences, compose a paragraph about the Brooklyn Bridge.

EXERCISE 29 *Go to the library, read some biographical material (get help from a librarian if you need it) about the Roeblings, and write a one-paragraph biographical sketch about them. Note: You should read the complete article about the Brooklyn Bridge from which we have excerpted this passage, in the* New York Times Magazine, *March 27, 1983, Section 6.*

Organization

5

Providing support in writing is one thing; organizing that support is quite another matter. You might have an excellent fund of specific details and still be frustrated about how to arrange them logically or to their best advantage. In the preceding chapter we touched on an aspect of organization in our discussion of the excerpt from Braudel's section on unemployment in the Middle Ages, yet we haven't really discussed outlining, which is the best and most effective method for organizing your materials.

The sort of paragraph we've been concerned with so far doesn't require much preliminary arrangement. You've simply made the specifics relate to the controlling idea in some sort of sequence. But as you make the transition from paragraph to essay, you'll need to be aware of the basic structure common to both. It's our theory that if you can organize a first-rate paragraph, you can also organize a short essay. In fact, we think that many a solid student paragraph could possibly be expanded into a short essay, an opinion we'll try to support in the next chapter. What we're saying, then, is that if you can write a solid, 150-word, factually supported paragraph that has unity, coherence, and good sentence structure, you can also write a short theme that has the same characteristics.

Outlining

In organizing a successful essay, you first need to outline the points you want to make and arrange them in order of importance. If you simply plunge in and try to handle too many ideas at once, you're likely to place small ideas where large ones belong and vice versa. But if you take time before you write to think about the relationships between ideas, you can save yourself some time and frustration. Actually, the outline can be likened to a tourist's guide, which aids you in arranging a rewarding trip. It gets you to the main points of interest without making unnecessary tours through the outback.

The proper form for an outline is indicated below. In our opinion, it's less confusing to place the thesis (or topic sentence, if you are making an outline for a single paragraph) and the conclusion *outside* the outline.

Thesis (or topic sentence): _____

I. _____ Primary Support

   A. _____ Secondary

      1. _____ Tertiary

      2. _____ Tertiary

   B. _____ Secondary

II. _____ Primary

   A. _____ Secondary

   B. _____ Secondary

      1. _____ Tertiary

      2. _____ Tertiary

   C. _____ Secondary

      1. _____ Tertiary

      2. _____ Tertiary

III. _____ Primary

   A. _____ Secondary

   B. _____ Secondary

Conclusion: _____

The outline form is marked by various divisions, as shown above. The divisions labeled by roman numerals provide the major or principal support for the thesis or topic sentence. The capital letter categories provide secondary support for each of the primary divisions. This secondary support is in turn developed by tertiary support, labeled by arabic numerals. One could continue this process of division still further, but unless you are writing a term paper or a complex essay, to divide further might create confusion.

The structure of the outline represents the proper positioning of smaller ideas in relation to larger, more significant ones. The thesis or topic sentence contains the dominant idea—the larger idea—and it is expressed in the form of a generalization. The primary support is also a generalization, but it is narrower and more focused than the thesis it supports. The secondary and tertiary support represent the specifics—the small ideas—that develop the larger thoughts. This last level is the "nuts and bolts" of the essay or paragraph. Thus, the outline demonstrates that old principle of subordination—proper thoughts in proper places—that we discussed in Chapter 2.

Classifying

The outline also demonstrates the principle of *classification,* one of the most important concepts used in any organizing process. Classification is the process by which larger bodies of information are divided into smaller related groups on the basis of some principle of categorizing. We might demonstrate the concept of classification as it operates in an outline with the following example. Suppose the writer had decided to write a paper on Napoleon and the effect he had upon shaping the Europe of his time. Perhaps one paragraph would describe certain facets of Napoleon's personality that lent themselves to great personal and national aims. The writer might begin by jotting down a series of facts accumulated through reading and research into the subject:

1. As a child in Corsica, Napoleon Bonaparte would always "take command" as the general in the military games he and his brothers played on their farm.
2. At his son's birth in 1811, Napoleon proclaimed the infant, King of Rome, adding, "I hope he will fulfill his destiny."
3. Napoleon commissioned artist Jacques Louis David to paint a grandiose portrait of the ceremonies at which he had himself crowned Emperor of France—an artistic record of a moment of French destiny.
4. Napoleon's sister Eliza was made Grand Duchess of Tuscany; his sister's husband, General Murat, became King of Naples.
5. By Napoleon's command, Paris fountains flowed with wine at his crowning in Notre Dame Cathedral, his way of sharing France's triumph with her citizens.
6. When angry, Napoleon would strike a subordinate; he knocked one general's head against a stone wall and struck another with his riding crop.
7. Like Charlemagne before him, Napoleon Bonaparte ordered a pope to preside at his coronation in 1804, a tribute to *la gloire de France.*
8. A young artillery lieutenant, Napoleon dreamed of leading an army across the Alps as Hannibal had done against ancient Rome.

9. Napoleon made his older brother Joseph, King of Spain, his younger brother Louis, King of Holland.
10. Early in life Napoleon had a conviction that he was "a superior being"; as a military cadet he fantasized about becoming another Caesar.

This list of facts, although interesting, hardly constitutes an organized body of information. The first task the writer has, then, is to organize and classify the facts—that is, divide them into appropriate categories.

In this instance, the various facts might best be organized into categories according to the points they make about the famous soldier/ruler. Each category classifies a way in which his ego asserted itself. For example, sentences 1, 8, and 10 reveal his early fantasies about military fame, fantasies in which he often links himself with leaders of the classical past. Sentences 3, 5, and 7 show Emperor Napoleon attempting to tie his personal identity to the glory of France. Sentences 2, 4, and 9 illustrate how he tried to rule his conquests through his family—an extension of self. Sentence 6 is difficult to fit into the writer's principle of classification; there is no other evidence of Napoleon's cruelty toward subordinates. Sentence 6 might thus be set aside, perhaps to be used later in some other part of the essay.

The writer will now try a tentative outline, beginning wth a topic sentence.

Topic Sentence: Many of Napoleon's actions and dreams reveal his surpassing ego and his sense of personal and national destiny: self, nation, family.

  I. His early fantasies link with a vision of the future.
     A. 1
     B. 8
     C. 10
 II. As emperor, Napoleon identified his power with the glory of France.
     A. 3
     B. 5
     C. 7
III. Napoleon ruled Europe through his family—an extension of himself.
     A. 2
     B. 4
     C. 9
Conclusion: In the light of evidence of such overwhelming ambition, it is not surprising that we label "Napoleonic" any personality that fulfills itself through the quest for power or grandeur.

The writer might have even more specifics concerning Napoleon's commanding personality, of course, and they could also be included. But if they were too numerous, the writer might have to distribute them over two paragraphs to ensure against excessive paragraph length. In essay writing, there is no law against writing two paragraphs on one aspect of a topic, provided that aspect is sufficiently important (and the role Napoleon's ego played in shaping the Europe of his time is certainly important).

As can be seen, the writer has classified into three equally important categories the ways that Napoleon's ego manifested itself and then positioned each specific from the list in its appropriate category. Failure to determine which are the major, or general, ideas and which are the minor, or specific, ideas can result in an outline like the following one, which fails to develop quality:

I. Fantasized about greatness.
   A. Wanted to cross Alps like Hannibal.
   B. Saw himself as a new Caesar.
II. The pope presided at the coronation to further French glory.
   A. Commissioned coronation painting to commemorate French moment.
   B. Provided fountains of wine to share success with Parisians.
III. Appointed his family to rule Europe.
   A. Brother Joseph crowned King of Spain.
   B. Sister Eliza made Grand Duchess of Tuscany.

In the above outline, division II is not organized correctly. It is not properly coordinated with divisions I and III. It is a *specific fact,* whereas the other two primary categories are focused generalizations, as they should be. The statement that appears above as division II should therefore be placed in the category of secondary support and labeled with a capital letter. It illustrates the generalization that Napoleon identified his personal power with national destiny.

A few additional hints about the setup and wording of outlines may help to prevent errors. Instructors of writing generally agree that each category of an outline should have at least *two* divisions to ensure adequate development. Thus, if you have a Roman numeral one, you must have a Roman numeral two. If you have A under I, you must also include B. You may, of course, have more than two categories, but you should try for *at least* two. It never hurts to have a bit more information than you need to write a paragraph or a paper.

Since the similar divisions of an outline are *coordinate* (of equal rank), they should also be grammatically parallel. Below is an example of an outline in which the writer has failed to provide division headings that are grammatically parallel.

I. Early power fantasies.
   A.
   B.

II. Nationalistic and egocentric.
   A.
   B.
III. Napoleon practiced nepotism.
   A.
   B.

Obviously, the first category heading is simply an abstract noun, which is perfectly acceptable. Division II, which should then also be a noun, is stated instead as two adjectives. Division III is expressed still differently, as a short sentence. All three should be *coordinate* and *parallel* in their grammatical structure. One possibility might be as follows:

  I. Napoleon's ambition
 II. His nationalism
III. His nepotism

The simplicity of the above does not necessarily diminish its usefulness. Here is another, perhaps fuller, possibility:

Topic sentence: Throughout his life, Napoleon expressed his grand ego in dream and in deed.

  I. He had early fantasies about future personal/national greatness.
   A. Saw himself as another Caesar.
   B. Dreamed of crossing the Alps, like Hannibal before him.
 II. Upon succeeding, he combined egotism with nationalism.
   A. Commanded a pope to preside at French coronation.
   B. Commissioned a painting to commemorate great French moment.
III. As emperor of the French, he ruled Europe through his family.
   A. Appointed brother Joseph King of Spain.
   B. Assigned sister Eliza to govern Tuscany.

Notice that the secondary supports are also grammatically coordinate and parallel in the above outline. The writer needn't follow the exact wording of the outline when writing the essay itself but should follow the direction taken by the outline. If the outline has unity and its categories are grammatically coordinate, those characteristics ought to be reflected in the structure of the writing. If you take the time in your outlines to work out the relationships among ideas of varying degrees of importance, you will save yourself valuable time in writing a final paragraph or essay. You will also ensure of a reasonable *singleness of purpose* in your writing. Another advantage of preparing an outline for your essay is that you can add to an outline if something important should occur to you after you begin to plan, and this will not necessitate rewriting the entire essay.

By this stage in your development as a planner and writer, you should be able to relax the rigid rule we made regarding the necessity for main clause unity. As long as each sentence (either in its independent or subordinate parts) contributes to the point of the paragraph, it could be said that singleness of purpose exists in the writing. You should also be able to make an outline for *anything* you intend to write about. (*Any* subject can be organized—and outlining is the key to that organization—in a paragraph, an essay, an article, a master's thesis, or a doctoral dissertation.)

SUMMARY

1. The outline represents a method of dividing or classifying a large body of facts into smaller related bodies.
2. The outline should be divided into primary categories, represented by roman numerals, and secondary categories, represented by capital letters. Further division is also possible and sometimes necessary.
3. The topic sentence and the conclusion should appear *outside* the outline.
4. The topic sentence represents large ideas; primary support represents medium-sized ideas; and secondary and tertiary support represents small ideas.
5. Equal categories of the outline should be worded in a grammatically parallel way; they must be *coordinate* in the outline, although you needn't follow the exact wording of the outline when writing the finished paper.

EXERCISE 30 *Ideally, an outline represents a descent from general to specific. In each of the following groups, the statements range from very general to very specific. In the blank, write the letters in order of descent from the most general to the most specific.*

1. a. It's often safer to be satisfied with what one has than to abandon it for what is difficult to retain.
   b. Latrina Ledesma broke off her engagement to her devoted longtime boyfriend, Euphemio Paz, in favor of a handsome actor traveling through Caracas.
   c. A bird in the hand is worth two in the bush.
   d. Ernesto Pajaro flew off to Mexico City with his acting troupe. Euphemio Paz refused to return Latrina's apologetic phone calls.

   Order of descent: _____

2. a. Red sky at morning is a sailor's warning.
   b. Cyril Gulassa ran down the back stairs just as the shore patrol was coming up the front; they did not meet.
   c. When dawn woke Bosun's Mate Third Class Cyril Gulassa in a cheap room in Hong Kong, he decided it was time to move—especially since he was absent without leave (AWOL).
   d. There are those who react to danger in intuitive ways.

   Order of descent: _____

3. a. One should try not to work faster than safety and efficiency dictate.
   b. Lisa Jo Giambetti lost her job at Repento's Restaurant for spilling a carafe of *vin rose* and three plates of linguini on a lady's lap.
   c. Haste makes waste.
   d. The headwaiter at Repento's Restaurant tried continually to persuade daring waitress Lisa Jo Giambetti to carry less pasta and make more trips.

   Order of descent: _____

4. a. An ounce of prevention is worth a pound of cure.
   b. A rainstorm during the fifth act of *Macbeth* soaked Cedric Cinchworth so thoroughly that he spent a month in Stanford Hospital with pneumonia.
   c. Occasionally, the homeliest safeguard is the most effective.
   d. Cedric Cinchworth refused to bring an empty plastic trash bag to the outdoor Shakespeare performance, as his instructor advised— an impromptu raincoat in case of heavy weather.

   Order of descent: _____

5. a. Yoshiki Kondo is tall for a bantamweight; he has long, scrawny arms and a tubercular-looking chest.
   b. It's difficult to estimate some men's power by their physical appearance.
   c. Yoshiki Kondo of Osaka, Japan, has knocked out thirty-seven of the thirty-nine men he has fought.
   d. You can't judge a book by its cover.

   Order of descent: _____

6. a. A stitch in time saves nine.
   b. A wet Peruvian April sent Frequencio Paredes's house sliding down the mountain into Lake Titicaca.
   c. Some people never seem to react promptly enough to avert misfortune.

d. Frequencio Paredes ignored his wife's constant reminders that the storm drains needed cleaning.

Order of descent: _____

7. a. Natalie Foxglove bought an "industrial strength" vacuum cleaner from a traveling salesman who said it would revolutionize housework and transform her home.
   b. Penny wise, pound foolish.
   c. Buying a reputable-quality product can often save you money in the long run.
   d. The machine tore loose from Natalie's grasp and ripped through a wall, shredding her Navajo rug and upsetting her China cabinet.

Order of descent: _____

8. a. Some people have lasting difficulties over a significant rebuff.
   b. When her fiancée broke their engagement to pursue his career as a rock musician in Naples, Eleanora Milobar hid in the wine cellar for a year.
   c. Once burned, twice shy.
   d. Eleanora Milobar vowed that any man who wished to marry her must first sign a holy contract placing all his legal and personal rights in her hands and forfeiting to her all the money he will ever make.

Order of descent: _____

9. a. Vito Rubella owns a fifty-acre Mendocino County swamp that has been described as "smelling like an open sewer."
   b. Vito Rubella looked at color photos of fifty acres of "prime vacation property" offered by Skipjack Developments Incorporated.
   c. One should never be attracted by appearances alone.
   d. All that glitters is not gold.

Order of descent: _____

10. a. The pool supervisor kept warning 110 pound lifeguard Catherine Karrer to use the prescribed technique of first throwing a tube—rather than jumping in—when attempting a rescue.
    b. Tried and true are best for you.
    c. There are well-tested methods for safely accomplishing any kind of undertaking.
    d. Lifeguard Catherine Karrer was dragged to the bottom and nearly drowned by a 300 pound man who panicked in the deep end. It took four strong adults to bring the two to safety.

Order of descent: _____

EXERCISE 31   *Try to divide each of the following subject areas into at least three major categories. If you know more than three categories, list them.*

1. Major sources of energy

   a. _____   d. _____

   b. _____   e. _____

   c. _____   f. _____

2. Major religions

   a. _____   d. _____

   b. _____   e. _____

   c. _____   f. _____

3. Kinds of medical doctors (or kinds of medicine practiced, for example, geriatrics)

   a. _____   d. _____

   b. _____   e. _____

   c. _____   f. _____

4. Major arts

   a. _____   d. _____

   b. _____   e. _____

   c. _____   f. _____

5. Major sciences

   a. _____   d. _____

   b. _____   e. _____

   c. _____   f. _____

6. Major types of music

   a. _____   d. _____

   b. _____   e. _____

   c. _____   f. _____

7. Major mass media

   a. _____   d. _____

   b. _____   e. _____

c. _____   f. _____

8. Major threats to the environment

   a. _____   d. _____

   b. _____   e. _____

   c. _____   f. _____

9. Kinds of lawyers

   a. _____   d. _____

   b. _____   e. _____

   c. _____   f. _____

10. Kinds of football played throughout the world

   a. _____   d. _____

   b. _____   e. _____

   c. _____   f. _____

EXERCISE 32   *This exercise will give you practice in preparing an outline for a paragraph (or even a full-length essay, taken up in Chapters 6 and 7). Rearrange the following items in the form of an outline according to their logical order, just as you would if you were outlining your own paragraph. The topic sentence and the concluding sentence are included in the details. Use your own paper to make your outline; rather than writing each sentence, designate the sentence by its number, as shown in the following example.*

Example

1. 1848–1850 the Army in California lost 716 of 1,290 men to desertion.
2. One trooper remarked, "The struggle between *right* and $6 a month and *wrong* and $75 a day is rather a severe one."
3. In one month, San Francisco's population dropped from several hundred to a dozen or so.
4. Thousands of Mexicans trekked overland from Sonora or sailed from Mazatlan.
5. So many sailors jumped ship that Admiral Thomas Jones said, "It will be impossible for the United States to maintain any naval establishment in California."
6. Viewing the scene, one Sacramento merchant said, "The field is left half-planted, the house half-built and everything neglected but the manufacture of shovels and pickaxes."
7. Even the military succumbed to the lure of the diggings.
8. Said future General William T. Sherman of the gold rush, "Only lunatic asylums can affect a cure for the ills brought on by gold fever."

9. John Sutter reported that within three weeks all his staff had deserted the mill and gone to the fields.
10. Locals had first pickings and reacted quickly.
11. When gold was struck in California, society abandoned duty for the promise of wealth.
12. The strike also drew seekers from abroad.
13. Twenty-five hundred Hawaiians crowded onto vessels bound for San Francisco.

Topic sentence: 11 (society abandons duty for gold)
  I. 10 (local society)
    A. 3
    B. 9
    C. 6
 II. 12 (newcomers from abroad)
    A. 4
    B. 13
III. 7 (even soldiers and sailors)
    A. 1
    B. 2
    C. 5
Conclusion: 8 (General Sherman's "evaluation" of the situation)

Notice how the outline attempts to divide "society" into three categories. Try to distinguish the principle of division or categorization in each of the outlines found in these two exercises.

1.   1. Early in the book, Joad says to the truck driver, "Nothing ain't none of your affair except skinnin' this here bull-bitch along, and that's the least thing you work at."
    2. Joad is capable of violence.
    3. He also tells the driver, "That big old nose of yours been sticking out eight miles ahead of your face. You had that big nose goin' over me like a sheep in a vegetable patch."
    4. "Homicide," Joad tells another character. "That's a big word—means I killed a guy."
    5. Joad is brash, outspoken, even flippant.
    6. When he first meets Casy, Joad tells him, "I'll climb fences when I got fences to climb."
    7. At the beginning of The Grapes of Wrath, Tom Joad has much to discover about himself and the role he must play in the migration to California.
    8. "Hell," Tom says to Muley Graves, "if I seen Herb Turnbull comin' for me with a knife right now, I'd squash him with a shovel."
    9. "Now look-a-here, fella," Joad says to the one-eyed man at the

junkyard. "You got that dead-eye wide open—hangin' out like a cow's ass. And ya dirty, ya stink. Ya like it. Let's ya feel sorry for yaself."

10. Joad is uncommitted.
11. Along the road to California, Tom Joad begins to understand the necessity of relating to others in the migrant community.
12. On the road, when brother Al talks with Tom about responsibility, Joad replies, "I ruther jus'—lay one foot down in front of the other."

2. 1. A person who has little aptitude in science classes will break his heart trying to become a physician.
    2. As Alexander Pope once said of our predispositions, "All looks yellow to the jaundiced eye."
    3. If one is physically small, he should not ruin his life over his failure to become a football star.
    4. Fear usually prevents us from trying to do things we're actually capable of.
    5. Negative emotions constitute by far the most powerful and injurious mind set of all.
    6. Another mind set involves projecting our "colored" attitudes upon the world and others: self-fulfilling prophecy.
    7. To deal more productively with life, one should recognize and identify destructive mind sets in himself/herself.
    8. Anxiety is a "stopper" which will consistently freeze up one's energies.
    9. If one is predetermined to see his co-workers or classmates as unsympathetic, they probably will turn out to be unsympathetic.
   10. The most common mind set—unrealistic expectations—is based on self-misconception.
   11. Unless one recognizes, confronts, and dominates these negative mind sets, he/she will seriously limit the potential to learn.

3. 1. In conflict, the mounted Indian had a clear psychological edge over a man afoot.
    2. Mounted hunters could pursue and surround buffalo herds.
    3. Primarily, the horse increased the Indians' efficiency and mobility.
    4. The horse even influenced social status within some tribes.
    5. Ordinary Indians like Knife-in-the-Water became rich and powerful leaders through horse ownership.
    6. Skilled horsemen were often rewarded with beads, rifles, or moccasins.
    7. The feel of the horse obeying the man's will gave the rider a sense of power.
    8. With horses, Indians could raid distant tribes for plunder and captives.

9. The coming of the horse changed the lives of the Plains Indians in some significant ways.
10. The Indian who owned more than one horse controlled capital; the Indian who owned none was without influence.
11. Said one leader, "A horse can carry seven times what a dog can."
12. Among Indians, the change wrought by the horse was as great as the change that steam and electricity was to bring to whites.
13. Indians could pack up and move entire villages in a brief time.
14. The horse also altered the psyche of the plains people.
15. One chief told the soldiers, "On the plains, a man afoot is nothing; mounted, he is great."

EXERCISE 33   *Do exactly as you did in the preceding exercise.*

1. 1. He once wrote Amos Pinchot, "Dear Sir, when I spoke of the Progressive Party having a lunatic fringe, I had specifically you in mind."
    2. TR's four-volume major work *The Winning of the West* is still standard reading for scholars.
    3. TR actually invented the infinitive "to falsify."
    4. TR was an ingenious phrasemaker whom we daily quote.
    5. Paul Schullery calls Roosevelt's contribution "the finest contribution by a single author to our knowledge of bear habits and hunting prior to the work of William Wright."
    6. Perhaps TR is best remembered as a capable naturalist.
    7. TR was a prolific and straightforward correspondent.
    8. He penned over 150,000 letters.
    9. Theodore Roosevelt's writing continues to fascinate readers because of its range, learning, and inventiveness.
    10. His first major work, *The Naval War of 1812*, earned him an immediate reputation.
    11. Such gifted and wide-ranged prose makes TR as memorable a writer as he was a chief executive.
    12. In *Ranch Life*, TR's chapter on the bighorn sheep is still useful to biologists.
    13. He created the phrases "the Square Deal," "the wealthy criminal class," and "clean as a hound's tooth."
    14. The rugged TR coined the terms "mollycoddle" and "pussyfooting."
    15. TR was a celebrated historian.

2. 1. A half-week outing on one-man inflatable kayaks pits the individual against "The Trench," "Kanaka," and "The Devil's Toenail."
    2. The river is tame over the 16-mile stretch between the Klamath

River and the Scott River, with deep pools ideal for diving into from overhanging rocks.

3. California's swift-flowing Klamath is a river for all seasons.
4. Fall is fishing time on the Klamath.
5. Late spring on the Klamath is for swimming and picnicking.
6. At the mouth near Requa, sunny beaches littered with driftwood provide great settings for barbeques and fish bakes.
7. A major run of king salmon reaches Iron Gate Dam in October.
8. Recreation-minded Californians would be poorer for the absence of this versatile waterway.
9. In March, one can drive for miles along the river and see only an occasional inflatable drift-boat.
10. In winter the river rests.
11. In September, steelhead angling is good between Copco Lake and the Oregon border.
12. The Klamath River Highway is hit by slides in December, January, and February—minimizing traffic to the scenic places.
13. Big rafts equipped with outboards challenge the heaviest rapids.
14. Summer features boating, for which the Klamath is justly famous.

3.
1. His stories of Indians and hardships preserve for him—and inform others of—the grandeur of his achievements.
2. More seriously, Carl reacts defensively when at the breakfast table he shouts, "The time's over. Why can't he forget it?"
3. Even the old man's clothing—black broadcloth with Kid Congress gaiters—suggests dignity and responsibility.
4. The survival of Grandfather's self-concept depends on his preserving his past image as a pioneer trailblazer and wagonmaster.
5. Carl also ridicules his son Jody by calling the boy "Big Britches" and banishing him from the house.
6. Soon afterwards, Jody greets his Grandfather with dignity, attempting to match his stride to the old man's.
7. Steinbeck's "The Leader of the People" is concerned with the roles that people of the different generations must enact to fulfill the needs of their ego.
8. Jody's well-planned mouse hunt that he wishes to share with Grandfather is a boy's bid for power over the fate of smaller creatures.
9. Carl's insistence upon "giving permission for anything that happens on the ranch" demonstrates his assertiveness.
10. Grandfather also claims that he was the head of the "great, crawling beast" that was the Western Movement.
11. Thus, the story ultimately explores ego needs and the tendency to resist changes that endanger people's self-concepts at a particular stage in their lives.

12. Early in the story, Jody's revelation that a letter has arrived comes out of his desire to have importance on the ranch.
13. Jody attempts to establish a role which could lead to future status as a man.
14. Carl Tiflin's primary motivation is to defend his present authority over the ranch and its inhabitants.

EXERCISE 34   *Answer the following questions as thoughtfully as you can. Be prepared to discuss them in class.*

1. In number 3 in the preceding exercise, the **TS** is obviously sentence 7. The key concepts in the sentence are *roles, different generations,* and *needs of their ego.* Circle the three primary supporting sentences. Underline the key concepts in each sentence that help provide unity to the outline.
2. Can you discern a logical order working in the outline? What idea is it based upon? How does it help promotes coherence?

_____

_____

_____

3. In what ways does the concluding sentence come full-circle in the outline?

_____

_____

_____

4. Could this outline be used to write a full-scale essay (a multi-paragraph paper)? If so, how would you divide the essay?

_____

_____

_____

EXERCISE 35   *The following paragraphs are organized in a unified, logical way; organize an outline for each one. In composing your outline, divide the paragraph into primary, secondary, and, if necessary, tertiary support. Keep the topic sentence and conclusion separate from the categories of the outline.*

1. (1) Mermaids and sirens—female sea-creatures in myth and literature— have long stood for cruel beauty, seductive danger, or unattainable love. (2) Pre-Christian stories and legends emphasized the seductiveness and

treachery of these mysterious females. (3) Sirens used their irresistible music to lure sailors to their deaths on the rocks or in whirlpools. (4) According to the poet Homer, the Greek hero Ulysses ordered his men to bind him to the mast so that he could not respond to the sirens' song. (5) Even when they were finally Christianized, mermaids continued to symbolize danger to mortals. (6) To the pilgrim, the mermaid stood for the Satanic forces that abducted and destroyed Christian souls. (7) This conviction was echoed in a sermon by Clement of Alexandria, who warned mortals to "sail past the song: it works death." (8) When the Church released the mermaid to modern art and literature, she remained a force for pulling men down. (9) In a poem by Yeats, for example, a cruelly forgetful mermaid drags her human lover to his death in the depths. (10) Isobel Gloag's painting *The Kiss of the Enchantress* depicts a half-willing knight about to be wrapped in the snakelike coils of a fatal sea woman. (11) So while the mermaid often seems a malign figure who endangers men in poetry and legend, she is nevertheless an attractive symbol of the dangers of desire.

2. (1) Increasing population has threatened the peace and ecological stability of the National Parks. (2) The greatest distraction is automobile traffic. (3) It is incredible yet true that each summer over a million cars discharge their exhaust in California's Yosemite Valley alone. (4) Traffic at the entrance of Great Smoky Mountains Park backs up several miles to Gatlinburg, Tennessee. (5) Nearly as disconcerting as cars are the noise and clutter that accompanies civilization. (6) Snowmobiles snarl past campers in winter, and all during the summer the waterways are clogged with skiers being towed by roaring speedboats. (7) Along the shore, a litter of candy wrappers and beer cans cause park attendants to work full time clearing the mess. (8) The least obvious—but perhaps most dangerous—threat to the parks is wear and tear upon formerly remote wildlife areas. (9) The increase in four-wheel drive vehicles has endangered previously inaccessible spots. (10) Says Pete Kuehne, who works part time for the California system, "We've run motorcycles and jeeps out of places we thought only a goat could reach." (11) In one park in the Southwest, vehicles are expressly prohibited from leaving designated roads and parking areas. (12) Even backpacking—which has grown tenfold in popularity over the past decade—has caused unprecedented wear upon trails such as California's John Muir and Eastern America's Appalachian. (13) Relief for the woodlands does not appear imminent; the Park Service expects that by the mid-1980s over four million people a year will visit America's thirty-seven National Parklands.

3. (1) In Sir Richard Burton, the adventurer, Victorian England produced one of the nineteenth century's most versatile men. (2) For one thing, Burton was an explorer. (3) In 1856, he fought fever and insects to become one of the first two Europeans to see Africa's Lake Tanganyika. (4) During this trip, Burton also stumbled upon the source of the Congo River, a fact he realized only years later. (5) His stature as an explorer was matched by his reputation as one of England's finest anthropologists. (6) In his examination of the forbidden Moslem cities of Mecca and Medina, Burton reported with great objectivity on the mores and customs he observed there, including the institution of polygamy. (7) His travels to re-

mote cities on the Nile provided him with enough information on the erotic rituals of the East to later translate the tales from the *Arabian Nights*. (8) To his other talents Burton added an unparalleled mastery of language. (9) He had at his command some thirty dialects from northern and central Africa. (10) These tongues ranged from Kanuri and Oji to Jolo. (11) Besides these, Burton spoke Arabic fluently enough to delight the king of Egypt at an Alexandria ball. (12) In his spare time, Burton also mastered at least six European languages, including French and Italian. (13) Such multiple talents, of course, made Burton a giant among Victorians and a biographer's dream.

EXERCISE 36   *Arrange the following details in a topic outline containing three roman numeral categories. We'll provide you with a start in devising the roman numeral headings.*

Thesis: Some of his accomplishments may be controversial, but Alfio Crema has always been one of the most versatile people around.

1. He won the 1965 Joseph Henry Jackson award for the most promising young California novelist.
2. He has published over thirty critical studies on authors like Mark Twain, Faulkner, and Camus.
3. His academic feats are impressive.
4. Crema is tremendously creative.
5. Crema once knew the tough workaday world.
6. His present occupation is questionable.
7. Crema once worked as a cub reporter on a newspaper in Evanston, Illinois.
8. At Northwestern University he lettered in boxing and ran distance in track.
9. He won the 1953 National Collegiate Cross Country Championships.
10. His collection of short stories entitled *Incredible Appetites* won him the Paris Review Award in 1982.
11. He has a Ph.D. in literature and has taught college in California.
12. He is alleged to have business connections with organized crime, but it has never been proved.
13. He is known recently to have won over a million dollars gambling; he has paid taxes on all his winnings.
14. He was an outstanding college athlete.
15. He was a fine prizefighter, once ranked seventh among pro middleweights.
16. His oil painting entitled *Sheepshead Bay* sold for over $30,000.
17. He lists his occupation as "real estate agent."
18. Crema once herded sheep on a ranch in Marin County, California.
19. He recently faced a Senate hearing on his alleged activities in importing and exporting—but was acquitted.

20. He once tried his hand at professional sports.
21. He played briefly in the PGA, winning two professional golf tournaments.
22. He has written a best-selling novel entitles *Shore of the Wide World*.
23. When he was seventeen, he went to sea with the Merchant Marines, serving five years.

Conclusion: Crema believes that a man should never get caught up in routine, which "kills us while we're still young."

Thesis: Some of his accomplishments may be controversial, but Alfio Crema has always been one of the most versatile people around.

I. *His academic and artistic credentials are impressive.*
    A.
       1.
       2.
    B.
    (and so on)

II. _____
    A.
    (etc.)

III. _____

The Form of the One-Paragraph Essay

6

To prepare ourselves for the expansion of the one-paragraph paper into a complete essay—let's say a five-paragraph paper—we need to take another look at the form of the one-paragraph paper. Perhaps it may be easier for us to visualize this form if we give it an actual, physical structure. The topic sentence, of course, begins the structure. This is so because, as we learned in Chapter 1, the topic sentence contains the dominating idea of a paragraph. We also learned that the dominating idea is a generalization and that the ideas that develop or explain it are specific, concrete statements. Another way of expressing the relationship between the generalization and the specific statements is to say that the dominating idea is the big idea, or the broad idea, and that the specific statements are smaller, or narrower, ideas. We can then illustrate the relationship between general-big-broad and specific-small-narrow by actually giving a paragraph a spatial shape.

Shaping the Paragraph

Each of the four statements in the structure on the next page is smaller or narrower than the generalization, or the big idea, in the topic sentence—not because we have put them in that particular position, but because each of them focuses on one of the four specific, concrete (or small, narrow) aspects making up the one general statement or big idea of the exciting Dr. Swackhammer.

| Topic sentence (big idea) | Professor Swackhammer is an exciting lecturer. |

1. 1. If anyone is still asleep in this big lecture hall at eight in the morning when Dr. Swackhammer begins his class in first year biology, the professor's voice soon wakes him/her up. It is a powerful bass, and the professor has an actor's control of it. He can make it roar like a lion or purr like a kitten.

2. 2. And if his voice isn't enough he can overwhelm you with his body. He is six feet two inches tall and weighs 270 pounds, but he doesn't look fat. In simple fact, he looks like a grizzly bear. And can he use that body! He can charge across the stage like an enraged, oversized fullback, he can lean over the lectern until you think both it and he are going to fall off the stage, or he can suddenly pick up that lectern, brandish it around as if it were nothing but a big pillow that he's going to hurl at the hundreds of students in the hall for being so young and so dumb. Or he can run around the stage, cavorting like a lightweight in a crazy dance, imitating a silly butterfly going after nectar, and bring the whole house down.

3. 3. And even his hair he makes use of. His bushy black eyebrows he can wiggle or make stand straight out, and his long black curly hair he can toss out and down in front of his face in one of his charges across the stage, pretending he's a buffalo.

4. 4. And finally his timing and the coordination of his physical antics with his rhetoric is just about perfect. When he wanted to emphasize that cells reproduce by division he leaned way down over the lectern, wiggled his eyebrows, shook his mane of hair, and then standing as stiff as a statue slowly repeated three times in a high falsetto stage whisper the word *divide*, and at the last divide he pushed his hairy right fist slowly at us as if he were gently forcing the word into our brains.

If we look at the paragraph more critically we see that, although its shape approximates a T-square, this is not quite the shape that we want.

Something is lacking; the T-square shape is right as far as it goes, but it ends too abruptly. And that, of course, is exactly the trouble; it is chopped off, truncated. Look at small idea number 4. You will immediately see that it is not an ending, a conclusion; it's merely one more small idea, and there is no real reason for stopping the paragraph at this point, other than that the writer simply ran out of gas. But that is not a good enough reason. Your paper should end only when you have provided sufficient support to validate the big idea, thereby satisfying the reader's curiosity and laying all doubts to rest. The end must always be accompanied by a signal to the reader that you think you have done these things and that you are now winding it up. Your conclusion rounds off the whole paragraph and completes its form. It is the last of the three basic parts—beginning, middle, and end.

Concluding the Paragraph

Fortunately, most of us have an inborn sense of form, and at the very least, a lack of form or a distortion of it makes us feel uneasy. We want books, stories, essays, jokes, and even one-paragraph papers to have form. If you pay attention to the twinge of uneasiness that you feel when you see something unfinished or formless (shapeless), you should be able to recognize formlessness even in your own writing.

Now to return to Dr. Swackhammer. Since we have already expressed the controlling idea in our topic sentence, we have our *beginning*, and because we have expressed our small ideas in specific statements, we have our *middle*, and the hardest work is over. What remains to be done—to add a conclusion or an *end*—is a relatively simple matter. All we must do now—and essentially this is how all conclusions are arrived at—is sum up, recapitulate the small ideas to recall the reader's attention to our big idea. We must echo the big idea, restate it, say simply in one way or another, "and now because of what I have shown you in my small ideas, you can see the validity of my big idea—how exciting Professor Swackhammer's biology class is." Naturally, we are not going to say it in quite these words, but we will say something that adds up to that. Sir James Jeans ends his classic essay (in which he tells us why the sky is blue) with a brief summary of the body of his paper and the statement "That is why the sky is blue."

By now, perhaps, you are beginning to guess that if a paragraph with a beginning and a middle is shaped like a T, then a paragraph with a beginning, a middle, and an end will be a T crossed at the bottom as well as at the top (a double-crossed T)—or an I, or the cross section of an I-beam, whichever you prefer.

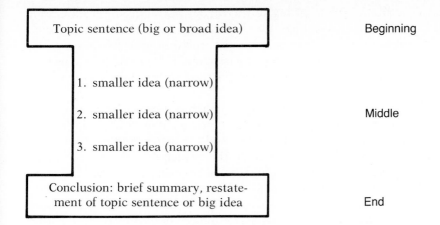

Topic sentence (big or broad idea)	Beginning
1. smaller idea (narrow)	
2. smaller idea (narrow)	Middle
3. smaller idea (narrow)	
Conclusion: brief summary, restatement of topic sentence or big idea	End

And now to fill in the bottom crosspiece. Since the paragraph is not very long, you could perhaps merely say:

> Wow! Is old Swackhammer ever exciting.

You might, however, wish to sum up the specific ideas with a more formal ending:

> Beyond any doubt, Dr. Swackhammer's physical attributes, his skilled actor's use of them, and his perfect coordination of them with his subject matter make him about the most electrifying teacher I have ever had.

Another variation might go like this:

> So any way you look at it, Dr. Swackhammer is an exciting teacher. His physical presence and manner compel your attention and his use of them to punctuate his rhetoric excites your mind.

Often a conclusion may briefly summarize the small ideas and echo the big ideas without referring directly to them:

> At any rate, old Swackhammer is a wild and crazy guy, and you'll never fall asleep in his class.

Notice that the statement *a wild and crazy guy* deftly reminds us of reasons that make Swackhammer exciting or in other words guarantee why you will not fall asleep. And usually the defter the better. Unfortunately, we cannot always be deft. Our deftness might have the wrong tone or we may simply want to repeat our basic ideas by briefly spelling them out in the conclusion. So we are often stuck with words and phrases such as *hence, therefore, so you see, and in short,* as stodgy as they may sound to us. However, the conclusion is the last thing the reader sees, so any ending that does the job of recalling to the reader both our small ideas and our big idea will usually suffice. We should remember that a simple ending, good enough for Sir James Jeans, is probably good enough for us, most of the time. "That is why the sky is blue." It's simple and it works. It would make for a dull conclusion only if you had nothing to say in the first place.

We can see, then, that it doesn't make much difference how we organize our conclusion, as long as we have one and as long as it accomplishes two jobs—summarizing the small ideas and restating the big idea—both of which are an unmistakable signal to the reader that the paragraph is ending. We can also see that, aside from completing the meaning of the paragraph, the conclusion helps to satisfy our esthetic sense, of which our sense of form is a part. What is shapeless or truncated offends us. What is complete and well formed pleases us, for a piece of writing has the power to please through its form as much as any physical object does. Even in a one-paragraph paper—the shortest and simplest piece one can write—we should always keep in mind the importance not only of the meaning, but of the form as well. In a piece of writing, meaning and form blend into each other and become indistinguishable. It is only to study what makes a piece of writing work that we separate the form from the meaning. Usually they work together, each heightening, each perfecting the other—if we let them.

To help us appreciate the importance of form in its relationship to meaning, let's turn once more to old Swackhammer and put just the bare bones of the ideas into our I-shaped paragraph. Notice that there are small ideas that follow each of the numbered ideas. What level of support or category of items in the outlines in Chapter 5 do these correspond to?

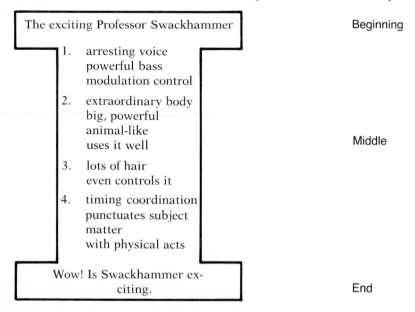

The advantage of placing a paragraph inside a diagram for practice is that it helps us to visualize the difference in size of the various thoughts and parts of a paragraph or essay. Most of us need to see with our eyes in order to "see" with our minds. A diagram before your eyes will help you to place ideas in their appropriate relationship.

SUMMARY

1. The big idea or generalization or dominating idea is a part of your beginning or your introduction. It crosses the T at the top. It begins the form.
2. The small ideas or the specific, concrete statements that develop your big ideas make up the column of the T or I. Often three or four of them are just about right. This makes up the middle part, or body, of the paragraph or essay.
3. The brief reference to your small ideas and the restating of your big idea—the summing up—widens your paper out again to make the bar that crosses the T at the bottom and completes the I. This is the ending or conclusion. It rounds off and completes your form.
4. Remember:

BEGINNING

Middle
Middle
Middle

E   N   D

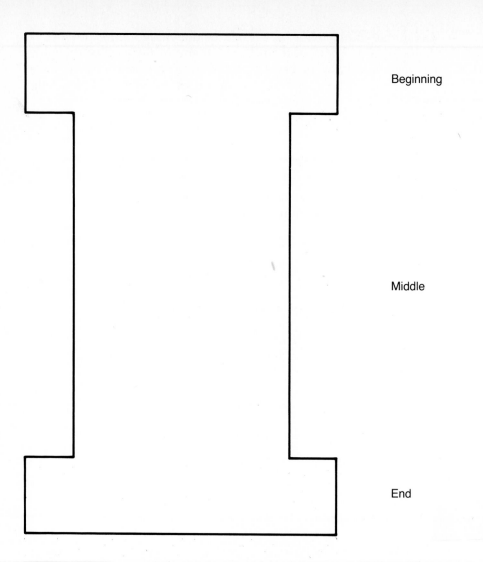

Beginning

Middle

End

EXERCISE 37   *In the I-shaped space above, place in the appropriate positions the items from your outline of one of the paragraphs in Exercise 35.*

The resemblance between outlining and placing the topic ideas of a paragraph in an I-shaped figure probably had occurred to you before you did this exercise. Now, of course, the resemblance is quite plain. However, seeing the topics inside a spatial shape may help you to understand better the principles of outlining. Placing topics inside an I-shape might serve as a substitute for outlining. Whatever you think about this, just remember that any kind of technique or device that you use is worthwhile if it helps you to understand the relationship between form and meaning and if it thereby enables you to write better than you did before.

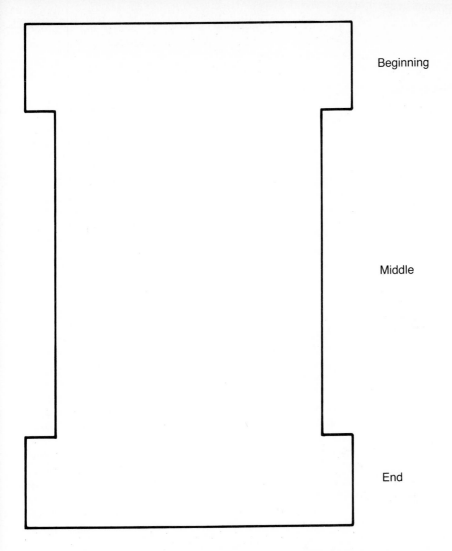

Beginning

Middle

End

EXERCISE 38   *In the I-shaped space above, write in the top crossbar the follow-ing topic sentence:* Each of Olaf Torgerson's three children resembles him in some way. *In the column (middle part) of the diagram write down a few brief ideas that show these resem-blances and number them 1, 2, and 3.*

Example: 1. Trygg has his father's powerful but graceful build.
2. Peter has his father's craggy but thoughtful face.
3. Looie has his father's strong but sensitive hands.

   Then, in the bottom crossbar write a conclusion.

Example: By build, face, and hands, each shares something of Olaf Tor-gerson. Some part of the man is reborn in each son.

You may, of course, make the children boys or girls and give them any names you like; and of course take any tone you please—serious, humorous, or whatever.

EXERCISE 39   *On your own paper, make and label an I-shaped diagram. Then write in the diagram a paragraph of about 150 words based on the Olaf Torgerson topic sentence. Make sure your paragraph has a beginning, middle, and end. Remember, for children you may substitute either girls or boys or make any other changes that might be more suitable for whatever you want to say about the Torgersons. A word of caution: form and the classification of ideas into big, little, or otherwise are not substitutes for thought. The awareness and use of form and organization will help you to think; they will not replace thinking. The variety of things you can say about Olaf and his three children is almost infinite; but don't get carried away. Remember that the qualities in the offspring that you are tracing to their father must make some kind of sense, if not on a serious level, then at least on a humorous one. So don't forget to use your common sense.*

EXERCISE 40   *Examine some object in either the natural or the man-made world, such as a leaf, tree, dog, cat, or fish, an ocean wave, stream, or river, a tennis racquet, football, baseball mitt, ski, matchstick, bridge, airplane, or whatever. Look at it closely and describe it in writing. Do more, however, then merely describe it. On your own paper, draw an I-beam shape and in about 150 or 200 words show how the shapes of the object and of its parts relate to their uses, functions, or purposes. Make sure you have a topic sentence at the beginning, a conclusion at the end, and sufficient detail in the middle or body to satisfy your readers' curiosity about the object. You should aim here at the target of describing the object so carefully and intelligently that readers will recognize it when they see it, even if they had never seen it before, or that they will see it better than they have ever seen it, no matter how familiar it might be.*

For example, if you wanted to write about a plant you might carefully pull or dig out of the ground a stalk of wild grain or a weed, with its roots. You would see how perfectly shaped the root system is, with its tiny hair-fingers and larger arms and shoulders, to extract nourishment from the soil and to anchor the plant to the ground. You might want to restrict yourself to describing only the root system in considerable detail, or in less detail you might describe the entire plant, showing how the shapes of the stalk, leaves and branches, and blossom or head are suited to their purposes. A reference book could help you by explaining the plant's nutritive, photosynthetic, and reproductive systems. The overall purpose of a tennis racquet or any man-made thing is usually clear enough, but the overall purpose of something in nature—including yourself—is indeed a different matter, the answer to which is usually rooted in your subjective self—in your religious and philosophical beliefs.

Experienced writers do not always write paragraphs that are shaped like I-beams. Often they use a short paragraph as a transition or bridge between two longer paragraphs, or as an introduction for a longer paragraph, or as an implied or stated conclusion for a preceding paragraph. But often even their longer paragraphs that, like ours, develop an idea are not shaped like I-beams. The topic sentence may be at the end, inductively, and serve as both main idea and conclusion, making an inverted T-shape (⊥). Or the topic sentence may be in the middle, producing a rectangular column, with a cross or bulge near the middle (+). Or sometimes there is no topic sentence at all; the main idea is implied rather than explicitly stated, and the reader infers the main idea or generalization from the mass of medium and small ideas. (What shape is this paragraph?)

EXERCISE 41 *Some of the following paragraphs are shaped like I-beams, others are not. Label the ones you think are I-beams with an I, in the space marked "shape." Find the topic sentence (it may not be at the beginning of the paragraph) and write the number of the sentence in the blank provided. Do the same for whatever sentence near the end that you think contains a clearly implied or explicitly stated conclusion. If you think a paragraph has no topic sentence or no concluding sentence, make up one that you think fits the paragraph and write it in the space provided. Indicate with a caret (ʌ) where in the paragraph it should go. Remember, in hunting for the topic sentence, look for a word or phrase that states the controlling idea.*

Example: (1) In an age of war and chaos, of doubt and wandering, the Benedictine monastery was a healing refuge. (2) It took dispossessed or ruined peasants, students longing for some quiet retreat, men weary of the strife and tumult of the world, and said to them, "Give up your pride and freedom, and find here security and peace." (3) No wonder a hundred similar Benedictine monasteries rose throughout Europe, each independent of the rest, all subject only to the pope, serving as communistic isles in a raging individualistic sea. (4) The Benedictine Rule and order proved to be among the most enduring creations of medieval man. (5) Monte Cassino itself is a symbol of that permanence. (6) Lombard barbarians sacked it in 589; the Lombards retired; the monks returned. (7) The Saracens destroyed it in 884; the monks rebuilt it; earthquake ruined it in 1349; the monks restored it; French soldiery pillaged it in 1799; the shells and bombs of the Second World War leveled it to the ground in 1944. (8) Today (1948) the monks of St. Benedict, with their own hands, are building it once more. (9) *Succisa virescit;* cut down it blooms again.

Shape: _____ **TS:** _____   Conclusion: _____

_____

_____

_____

In this paragraph from Will Durant's *The Age of Faith*, the historian is writing about the famous monastery of Monte Cassino, founded in 529 by St. Benedict in Italy, between Rome and Naples. Which sentence do you think is the topic sentence? Is the last sentence a conclusion? If so, is it implied or explicitly stated? Are there, perhaps, two sentences with topic sentence ideas in them? If so, could they be combined into one topic sentence? Discuss these questions with your instructor and with the rest of the class and then in class, fill in the blanks after the paragraph. Proceed now with the following paragraphs as instructed on page 121.

1. This paragraph is from the historical novel *The Hunchback of Notre Dame* by the nineteenth-century French writer Victor Hugo. He is writing about the hunchback (the *bell-ringer*) who is said to have lived in Notre Dame Cathedral in the late fifteenth century.

> (1) In process of time, the strongest attachment took place between the bell-ringer and the church. (2) Cut off forever from society by the double fatality of his unknown parentage and his misshapen nature, imprisoned from childhood within these impassable boundaries, the unhappy wretch was accustomed to see no object in the world beyond the religious walls which had taken him under their protection. (3) Notre Dame had been successively, to him, as he grew up and expanded, his egg, his nest, his home, his country, the universe.

Shape: _____ **TS:** _____   Conclusion: _____

_____

_____

_____

2. The following paragraphs are from "Who Killed Benny Paret," an article by the American writer Norman Cousins. Benny Paret, the world welterweight champion, was destroyed by a barrage of fearful blows to the head in the twelfth round of his fight in defense of the championship on the night of March 24, 1962, in Madison Square Garden. He went into a coma in the ring, never regained consciousness, and died shortly after. His opponent, Emile Griffiths, after the fight, said he had not meant to hurt Paret. The fight was televised and millions of people of all ages witnessed it.

> (1) In short, the investigators looked into every possible cause except the real one. (2) Benny Paret was killed because the human fist delivers enough

impact, when directed against the head, to produce a massive hemorrhage in the brain. (3) The human brain is the most delicate and complex mechanism in all creation. (4) It has a lacework of millions of highly fragile nerve connections. (5) Nature attempts to protect this exquisitely intricate machinery by encasing it in a hard shell. (6) Nature, however, can protect man against everything except man himself. (7) Not every blow to the head will kill a man—but there is always the risk of concussion and damage to the brain. (8) A prize fighter may be able to survive even repeated brain concussions and go on fighting, but the damage to his brain may be permanent.

(1) In any event it is futile to investigate the referee's role and seek to determine whether he should have intervened to stop the fight earlier. (2) That is not where the primary responsibility lies. (3) The primary responsibility lies with the people who pay to see a man hurt. (4) The referee who stops a fight too soon from the crowd's viewpoint can expect to be booed. (5) The crowd wants the knockout; it wants to see a man stretched out on the canvas. (6) This is the supreme moment in boxing. (7) It is nonsense to talk about prize fighting as a test of boxing skills. (8) No crowd was ever brought to its feet screaming and cheering at the sight of two men beautifully dodging and weaving out of each other's jabs. (9) The time the crowd comes alive is when a man is hit hard over the heart or the head, when his mouthpiece flies out, when the blood squirts out of his nose or eyes, when he wobbles under the attack and his pursuer continued to smash at him with pole-axe impact.

Shape: _____ TS: _____   Conclusion: _____

_____

_____

_____

3. This paragraph is from *Living Poor* by the American farmer and writer Moritz Thomsen. Full of humor, sorrow, and beauty, *Living Poor* is called "A Peace Corps Chronicle" by Mr. Thomsen, and recounts his experiences as a Peace Corps volunteer in Ecuador in the 1960s.

(1) Like flowers, their splendor fades quickly; before they are thirty their faces are transformed. (2) They have been defeated and the eyes are as guarded and cynical as the women's. (3) They have a foxy look; they have learned that you have to be sharp to stay alive and that you really can't trust anyone, and the sharpness shows through. (4) They have been corrupted by life, by searing cane alcohol, protein starvation, fevers, worms, and amoebas, and by the sufferings and deaths of their children. (5) At forty they are old.

Shape: _____ TS: _____   Conclusion: _____

_____

_____

_____

4. The article "I'll Never Escape the Ghetto" by the black lawyer Stanley Sanders contributed this paragraph. Sanders went to Oxford University from 1963 to 1965 as a Rhodes Scholar and later received a law degree from Yale University. *South Los Angeles* is another name for Watts, but carries less stigma; during a short period in his life Mr. Sanders gave that name rather than Watts for his home.

(1) I have affectionate ties to Watts. (2) I bear the same mark as a son of Watts now that I did during that oratorical contest in high school. (3) I may be personally less vulnerable to it today, but I am nevertheless influenced by it. (4) While a group in Whittier, California, may regard it as unfortunate that its college's first Rhodes Scholar comes from Watts, I, for my part, could not feel more pride about that than I do now. (5) I feel no embarrassment for those who think ill of Watts. (6) I had once felt it. (7) Now I only feel regret for once having been embarrassed. (8) "South Los Angeles" is a sour memory. (9) Watts is my home.

Shape: _____ **TS:** _____ Conclusion: _____

_____

_____

_____

5. This paragraph is from the essay "The Ridge-Slope Fox and the Knife Thrower" by the American writer Edward Hoagland.

(1) Once I read about a medieval death imposed by a potentate on two lovers. (2) He had their arms tied around each other and left them lying face to face to starve. (3) Supposedly the horror of it was that they would grow to loathe one another, sweating in the mockery of the coital position. (4) But I don't see it so; I remember my explorer friend shivering, hugging his ribs in a tent in New Guinea. (5) Recently two revolutionaries were hanged in the Near East, and as they twisted, blindfolded, their hands tied behind their backs happened to touch, and touching, clasped, and so they died grasping each other.

Shape: _____ **TS:** _____ Conclusion: _____

_____

_____

_____

6. This paragraph is from the book *Seven Pillars of Wisdom* by the English soldier-writer T. E. Lawrence, hero of the desert fighting in World War I. After the war he felt betrayed by his country's government because he thought they had reneged on promises made through him to the Arabs in return for the Arabs' help in fighting the Turks. A reckless motorcyclist as well as a reckless but brilliant military strategist, he was killed on a motorcycle in 1935.

(1) ". . . And we marched and we marched, and the land was barren, and we heard nothing. (2) And on our right hand came a man, a negro, on a donkey. (3) The donkey was grey, with black ears, and one black foot, and on its shoulder was a brand like this" (a scrabble in the air), "and its tail moved and its legs: Auda saw it, and said, 'By god, a donkey.' (4) And Mohammed said, 'By the very God, a donkey and a slave.' (5) And we marched. (6) And there was a ridge, not a great ridge, but a ridge as great as from the here to the what-do-you-call-it *(lil biliyeh el hok)* that is yonder: and we marched to the ridge and it was barren. (7) That land is barren: barren: barren."

Shape: _____ TS: _____ Conclusion: _____

_____

_____

_____

7. Out of Aleksandr Solzhenitsyn's *The Gulag Archipelago Two* comes this paragraph. Solzhenitsyn, Russian writer and dissident, twice-decorated soldier in the Russian army in World War II, was sentenced to two years in prison and eight years in an Arctic zone slave-labor camp for an unflattering remark about Stalin in a letter to a friend. After Stalin's death, he was freed in 1956, and he wrote at least seven books and numerous short works as well as poetry and drama exposing the prison and slave-labor camp system in the Soviet Union. In 1974 the government expelled him from the country. Solzhenitsyn is now living in the United States.

(1) One's own order to oneself, "*Survive,*" is the natural splash of a living person. (2) Who does not wish to survive? (3) Who does not have the right to survive? (4) Straining all the strength of our body! (5) An order to all our cells: Survive! (6) A powerful charge is introduced into the chest cavity, and the heart is surrounded by an electrical cloud so as not to stop beating. (7) They lead thirty emaciated but wiry Zeks three miles across the Arctic ice to a bathhouse. (8) The bath is not worth even a warm word. (6) Six men at a time wash themselves in five shifts, and the door opens straight into the subzero temperature, and four shifts are obliged to stand there before or after bathing—because they cannot be left without convoy. (7) And not only does none of them get pneumonia. (8) They don't even catch cold. (9) (And for ten years one old man had his bath just like that, serving out his term from age fifty to sixty. (10) But then he was released, he was at home. (11) Warm and cared for, he burned up in one month's time. (12) That order—"Survive!"—was not there. . . .)

Shape: _____ TS: _____ Conclusion: _____

_____

_____

_____

8. This paragraph is from "The Legend of Gregorio Cortez," a short story by the Chicano-American writer Americo Paredes, from his book *With His Pistol in His Hand,* his dissertation for the doctorate.

(1) He was a man, a Border man. (2) What did he look like? (3) Well, that is hard to tell. (4) Some say he was short and some say he was tall: some say he was Indian brown and some say he was blond like a newborn cockroach. (5) But I'd say he was not too dark and not too fair, not too thin and not too fat, not too short and not too tall: and he looked just a little bit like me. (6) But does it matter so much what he looked like? (7) He was a man, very much of a man: and was a Border man. (8) Some say he was born in Matamoros: some say Reynosa: some say Hidalgo, it's all the same Border: and short or tall, dark or fair, it's the man that counts. (9) And that's what he was, a man.

Shape: _____   **TS:** _____   Conclusion: _____

_____

_____

_____

9. This paragraph is from Chapter 22, "Feudalism and Chivalry," in Will Durant's *The Age of Faith.*

(1) The peasant's cottage was of fragile wood, usually thatched with straw and turf, occasionally with shingles. (2) We hear of no fire-fighting organization before 1250; when one of these cottages took fire it was usually a total loss. (3) As often as not the house had only one room, at most two; a woodburning fireplace, an oven, a kneading trough, table and benches, cupboard and dishes, utensils and andirons, caldron and pothanger, and near the oven, on the earthen floor, an immense mattress of feathers or straw, on which the peasant, his wife and children, and his overnight guest all slept in promiscuous and mutual warmth. (4) Pigs and fowl had the run of the house. (5) The women kept the place as clean as circumstances would permit, but the busy peasants found cleanliness a nuisance, and stories told how Satan excluded serfs from hell because he could not bear their smell. (6) Near the cottage was a barn with horse and cows, perhaps a beehive and a hennery. (7) Near the barn was a dunghill to which all animal or human members of the household contributed. (8) Roundabout were the tools of agriculture and domestic industry. (9) A cat controlled the mice, and a dog watched over all.

Shape: _____   **TS:** _____   Conclusion: _____

_____

_____

_____

10. In this passage an American couple travel through the North African desert in the back of a produce truck. Port, the woman's husband is seriously ill. The scene is from the novel *The Sheltering Sky* by the American writer and musical composer Paul Bowles.

(1) The truck roared on and on. (2) Fortunately the back was completely open, or the exhaust fumes would have been troublesome. (3) As it was she caught a sharp odor now and then, but in the following instant it was dissipated in the cold night air. (4) The moon set, the stars were there, she had no idea how late it was. (5) The noise of the motor drowned out the sound of whatever conversation there may have been in front between the driver and the mechanic, and made it impossible for her to communicate with them. (6) She put her arms about Port's waist, and hugged him closer for warmth. (7) "Whatever he has, he's breathing it away from me," she thought. (8) In her moments of sleep she burrowed with her legs beneath the sacks to keep warm; their weight sometimes woke her, but she preferred the pressure to the cold. (9) She had put some empty sacks over Port's legs. (10) It was a long night.

Shape: _____ **TS:** _____ Conclusion: _____

_____

_____

_____

11. This paragraph is from the chapter "The Objects of Love" in *The Art of Loving* by the humanist writer Erich Fromm. Compare the main idea in this paragraph with that in paragraph 5.

(1) Love is not primarily a relationship to a specific person; it is an *attitude*, an *orientation* of *character* which determines the relatedness of a person to the world as a whole, not toward one "object" of love. (2) If a person loves only one other person and is indifferent to the rest of his fellow men, his love is not love but a symbiotic attachment, or an enlarged egotism. (3) Yet, most people believe that love is constituted by the object, not by the faculty. (4) In fact, they even believe that it is a proof of the intensity of their love when they do not love anybody except the "loved" person. (5) Because one does not see that love is an activity, a power of the soul, one believes that all that is necessary to find is the right object—and that everything goes by itself afterward. (6) This attitude can be compared to that of a man who wants to paint but who, instead of learning the art, claims that he has just to wait for the right object, and that he will paint beautifully when he finds it. (7) If I truly love one person I love all persons. (8) I love the world. (9) I love life. (10) If I can say to somebody else, "I love you," I must be able to say, "I love in you everybody, I love through you the world, I love in you also myself."

Shape: _____   **TS:** _____   Conclusion: _____

_____

_____

_____

12. In this violent passage from the novel *The Family of Pascual Duarte* by the contemporary Spanish novelist Camilo José Cela, the protagonist, Pascual, out of a background of poverty and ignorance, unredeemed by hope, feels only murderous hatred for his enemy. Yet, in the next paragraph in the book, the hatred culminates in an embrace, although a deadly one.

> (1) I was cold-blooded as a lizard, at that moment. (2) I knew well enough what I was about and how far I would have to go. (3) I squared away, calculated the distance between us and, allowing for no further talk—so that what happened the time before should not happen again—I swung a stool right into the middle of his face. (4) He was hit so hard that he went over backwards and lay like a dead man up against the fireplace. (5) A moment later he struggled to get up, drawing his knife the while. (6) His face was full of malice, a fright to see. (7) But his shoulder bones had been crushed, and he couldn't really move. I grabbed hold of him and dragged him to the edge of the road, and there I pushed him down.

Shape: _____   **TS:** _____   Conclusion: _____

_____

_____

_____

13. This paragraph is from Arthur Koestler's book *The Thirteenth Tribe,* in which he develops the thesis that most of the Jewish people alive today are not Semitic in ethnic origin but rather, are descendants of Turkish tribes who made up the empire of the Khazars in Southern Russia between the Black and the Caspian Seas in A.D. 400–1000. Koestler was born and raised in Hungary, and died in London in 1983. A journalist, intellectual and novelist, he lectured at a number of American universities, and was a Fellow in the Behavioral Sciences at Stanford University in 1964–1965.

> (1) If I may add a personal observation—I frequently met on visits to the United States Central European friends of my youth who emigrated before World War Two and whom I had not seen for some thirty or forty years. (2) Each time I was astonished to find that they not only dressed, spoke, ate, and behaved like Americans, but had acquired an American physiognomy. (3) I am unable to describe the change, except that it has something to do with a broadening of the jaw and a certain look in and around the eyes. (4) (An anthropologist friend attributed the former to the increased use of the

128   The Form of the One-Paragraph Essay

jaw musculature in American enunciation, and the look as a reflection of the rat-race and the resulting propensity for duodenal ulcers.) (5) I was pleased to discover that this was not due to my imagination playing tricks—for Fishberg, writing in 1910, made a similar observation: ". . . The cast of countenance changes very easily under a change of social environment. (6) I have noted such a rapid change among immigrants to the United States. . . . (7) The new physiognomy is best noted when some of these immigrants return to their native homes. . . . (8) This fact offers excellent proof that the social elements in which a man moves exercise a profound influence on his physical features."

Shape: _____   TS: _____   Conclusion: _____

_____

_____

14. This paragraph comes from Stefan Zweig's *Balzac*, a biography of the French nineteenth-century novelist Honoré de Balzac. Mr. Zweig, an Austrian, died in 1942. Balzac was famous not only for the rapidity and carelessness with which he often wrote but also for the vast number of books he completed, many of which are still acclaimed as masterpieces by critics, readers, and writers.

(1) Language is a jealous master and avenges itself inexorably on every artist who even occasionally treats it with unconcern. (2) Balzac wakened too late to a sense of responsibility, and after he had reached maturity he would desperately go through his manuscripts, galleys, and page-proofs ten or twenty times; but it was too late to hoe out the weeds which had been allowed to take root with such impudent luxuriance. (3) If Balzac's language and style remained irredeemably defective, it was because he had been untrue to himself in the decisive years of his development.

Shape: _____   TS: _____   Conclusion: _____

_____

_____

15. This is part of a longer paragraph, which is the conclusion of a section in Braudel's *The Wheels of Commerce*. Most of the passage is Braudel quoting the famous French historian Jules Michelet (1798–1874).

No one has described better than Michelet how the industrial revolution was in the end a revolution in demand, a transformation of 'desires' to use Turgot's word, which might please some of today's philosophers. In 1842, Michelet writes, 'the cotton mills were in crisis. They were choking to death, as the warehouses were overflowing and there were no buyers. The panic-stricken mill-owners dared neither to work nor to stop work with their all-devouring machines . . . Prices fell, but that accomplished nothing; they fell yet again, until cotton was selling at six *sous* . . . then something unexpected happened. The sound of six *sous* seemed to act as a trigger. Millions of buyers, poor people, who had never bought [textiles, cotton] before, began to stir. And it could then be seen how powerful and immense a consumer the people can be when aroused. The warehouses were emptied in a flash. The machines went frantically back to work . . . And the result was a major, though little remarked revolution in France, a revolution in cleanliness and the suddenly improved appearance of the poor home: people had bed linen, body linen, linen for the table and windows: it was now possessed by whole classes who had never had any since the world began.'

Shape: _____   **TS:** _____   Conclusion: _____

_____

_____

_____

The Form of the Essay

7

By now you know that not all one-paragraph papers are shaped like a T crossed at top and bottom or like an I. Some one-paragraph papers are shaped like an inverted T($\perp$), with a bar at the bottom and none at the top. Others have nothing at top or bottom, but rather have a bar—or at least a bulge—somewhere in the middle (+). (Some have no shape at all; but, as you have probably noticed, they don't work very well.) At any rate, these other forms can work just as well as our T-shape, but unless you are an experienced writer, they are much more difficult to use.

After all, it is logical that the topic sentence should come first. Remember, your big idea is the guide. You look to it for direction. Everything you say must follow the line of thought introduced in the topic sentence. You cannot stray from the path of the subject of the big idea. Each of your small ideas develops the big idea by being about it or related to it. Also, with your topic sentence as the first sentence of your paragraph, it is easy to check to see if such a relationship actually exists. For example, if the big idea in your topic sentence is the thrill of body contact in football, you must talk about that particular thrill, not about some other one. But since it is so easy and pleasant to let our thoughts stray, we might find ourselves three-fourths of the way through our paper putting down something like this: "And then I'll never forget the fun of just being part of the gang in that old football squad at Union High." By now, if you have really tried to improve your writing, you have probably discovered that straying from the subject is easy. But you have also found out that with the topic sentence at the beginning, all you have to do to see that you're on the right track is simply to look back to that sentence and there it is, as plain as day. Being one of the gang on the squad may have been fun, but it isn't related closely enough to the kind of thrill described in your main idea. So cut it out of the paragraph; it doesn't belong. There is nothing wrong with it as an idea—but not for a paragraph about the thrill of body contact in football. This thought brings us to another and quite different kind of advantage in getting the main idea down at the beginning. The advantage is one of fertilization of our minds. It comes from the act of setting down main ideas and subordinate ideas, which is a way of getting ourselves started by concentrating on the material itself instead of on the way of writing about the material. We might say that it amounts to a kind of device that painlessly forces us to think about our ideas without the distractions of spelling, punctuation, sentences, and the rest of it. Concentrating on these things can come later. However, as we begin to write down our small ideas to develop our big ideas, we often run into difficulty for three basic reasons: (1) we are not interested enough in our subject; (2) we don't have enough information to develop our subject; (3) other ideas related to but not subordinate to the big idea keep forcing their way into our paper.

The solution to the first problem, lack of sufficient interest, is obvious: change your topic to fit what comes into your head most easily—that is, whatever you are really interested in. If, instead of the thrill of body contact, you keep recalling the bus ride home late at night with all the guys singing, then throw out the old topic and use the new one, the pleasures of being one of the gang.

In dealing with the second problem, lack of information, you have to be honest with yourself and admit that you didn't really have any right to choose that subject in the first place—simply because you didn't know enough about it. Instead, choose something that you have enough knowledge of to write about. If you still like your original big idea and have a hunch that it is a good one, you can work that out by going to the library for the information you need to back up and develop your big ideas.

The solution to the third problem is what this chapter is mainly about. First, however, we must clearly identify the problem. Often, an idea of equal importance to your big idea keeps cropping up, if not in your paper at least in your mind. You want to talk about both the fun of being part of the squad and the fun or satisfaction of achieving something either as an individual or as part of a team, whether in tennis, football, basketball, track, baseball, water polo, or whatever. Or maybe what had started out as a paper having as its main topic the misery of playing second fiddle to an older brother has turned into a paper on the combined miseries of being caught in the middle between Big Brother and Little Sister with Mom and Dad thrown in for good measure—the wealth of ideas and details depending on the depth and scope of your miseries. Then the more you look at these various gripes or miseries and really think about them, the more examples and incidents supporting and illustrating these ideas begin to crowd into your head. Put them all down on your paper where you can see them and keep going, listing all the things that bug you—Brother, Sister, Mom and Dad, car insurance, job, school, and the whole catastrophe. Then, if you are a serious student—that is, more interested in improving your writing than in expressing your miseries—you will realize at some point that your one-paragraph paper has become an impossibly crowded mess. So be it. Don't be alarmed. What has happened is that in your attempt to develop your big idea through specific and concrete statements, every detail you have written down has led you to recall several other related details. It seems as if everything has conspired to make you turn out ideas. What you now have is enough material to expand your one paragraph into five paragraphs.

Expanding the Paragraph

The main difference between the one- and the five-paragraph paper is in its scale; the overall form is the same. A five-paragraph paper stands in relation to a one-paragraph paper much as a heavyweight fighter stands in relation to a flyweight fighter: there is simply more to the big one.

Before we examine the mechanics of expansion, however, let's look at a student's one-paragraph paper that he later expands into a five-paragraph essay. First read the paper in its original, one-paragraph form in the I-shaped diagram on the next page.

Although I agree that sports are important to students, I believe that the experiences people have later in life are much more important to them than those of playing in the "big game."

Beginning

    1. One of the greatest of experiences in life is marriage. Here young people are tested in ways and to degrees that they'll never encounter in a football or basketball game. If a husband and wife are really in love with each other, they'll have a unity and teamwork superior to any squad's.

    2. Many valuable experiences also occur when people begin to earn a living. They soon learn the ups and downs of life as they enter into a competition that is tougher than any sport and that is played for higher stakes. If a person made too many mistakes in a game, no one suffered very much, but now, if the person is fired for making too many mistakes on the job, the whole family may suffer great privation.

Middle

    3. Then in their declining years the couple has the joy not only of their children but of their children's children and of growing old together.

So you see, the experiences of playing in the big game cannot compare in importance with the experiences a person has later on in life.

End

    We don't necessarily see what the writer wants us to see in his paragraph. Part of the trouble is that the subject is too big to be developed convincingly in one paragraph or in a mere 190 words. His three small ideas in the column of the I, though smaller than his major idea, are still too large and too general, lacking the concrete, specific detail to convince us that the writer knows what he is talking about. The second sentence in item 2, for example, is better, mainly because it begins to develop the first statement. But there isn't enough of this kind of material to make the paragraph work, and even the "ups-and-downs" statement is too general and undeveloped; there simply isn't enough room in such a short paper to provide the necessary specific detail to develop so many general statements. Because the writer was getting his ideas down, he was lulled into thinking that he was writing convincingly. But he wasn't—he was only including generalizations instead of giving specific examples that would illustrate the general statements.

The student, however, does have the fundamentals of a good essay. He has the skeleton, an outline of his ideas that he can expand into a multi-paragraph paper. He has five basic items: the beginning, the three middle items, and the end—five things finite and definite enough for him to focus on. He can make the expansion without any desperate floundering if he keeps in mind the relationship between the flyweight and the heavy-weight fighters and one- and five-paragraph papers. The following essay, representing the student's expansion of the one-paragraph paper, is the student's reply to an essay entitled "In Defense of the Fullback" by sportswriter Dan Wakefield.

IN DEFENSE OF LIFE

Beginning

1. I agree with Dan Wakefield in his standing up for sports in his essay "In Defense of the Fullback." However, I find myself opposed to his main idea that nothing we experience later on in life can compare in importance with our sports experiences in school. The expression used in describing the so-called glory was the fullback's "eighty-yard run," and the author makes it stand for the highest achievement in the athlete's life. Supposedly, the athlete will never again do anything else so great, and thus the rest of his life will seem very dull. I feel that just the normal living of life contains many experiences far greater than that of the "eighty-yard run."

Middle

2. One of the greatest of all experiences of life is marriage. Here young people are tested in ways and to degrees that they would never encounter in a football or basketball game. If a husband and wife are really in love with each other, they'll have a unity and teamwork superior to any squad's. The loyalty between husband and wife is based on a closer human relation-ship than the loyalty one team member owes to the other members. Raising children also brings with it experiences of all types. Looking at the children and knowing they are yours and that you must take care of them and raise them is a lot more challenging—and should be more satisfying—than four years of looking at the other members of the team on the field and around the campus. Many look at this time when their children are young and com-pletely dependent on them as the most cherished period of their lives. When Tad Jones (the Yale coach quoted in the Wakefield essay) made the state-ment that "the big game was the most important moment in a player's life," he must have been forgetting the pride a parent feels when he sees his son or daughter graduate from college or when he admires a portrait of his fam-ily. Certainly, experiencing marriage and family life is at least as thrilling as playing in the "big game."

3. Many valuable experiences also occur when people begin to earn a living. They learn the "ups and downs" of life and begin to realize what competition really is when they start working for keeps instead of playing for fun. This is part of the struggle of life, and the stakes are the family's welfare and the person's sense of self-worth. They learn the joy of doing a job well and being paid for it. As they progress in their jobs, they begin to experience the sense of their own value in the contribution that they make to the world. Gradually they see that their experience in sports was child's play in comparison with the events of their working career.

4. Another time when we experience many wonderful things is in our declining years. During this time we often become aware of the beauties of life. The falling of early snow or the sweet freshness of a spring day may be very dear to an aging person. A husband and wife growing old together share many fulfilling experiences, such, as spending time not only with their own children, but with their children's children.

5. Thinking, then, of the variety and seriousness of the experiences a person has throughout the course of marriage, work, and parenthood, you may agree with me that "eighty-yard runs" and playing in big games are insignificant child's play in comparison with the experiences of mature life.

Though the student has not been entirely successful in his expansion, this is obviously a much better paper than the one-paragraph paper. It is important to note that the faults of the longer paper are not due to its expansion. That was pretty easy: the student used the same form and simply enlarged it and subdivided its ideas to discuss them in more depth and detail. Rather, the faults of the longer paper are caused by the same sort of carelessness that was responsible for the faults in the one-paragraph paper. But notice that because of the clarity of form in the longer paper, no less than in the shorter paper (beginning, middle, end), the faults can easily be seen; we can isolate them and set to work eliminating them.

The errors and faults in the essay should be apparent to you, and you should be able to identify most of them. There are mechanical errors. The essay does not adhere to the principles of coherence and organization and subordination that we have already discussed. One of the paragraphs is better than the others. Throughout the essay the student fails to provide enough specific and concrete detail for the central idea. Nevertheless, there are some strengths in the essay—an important one being the writer's enthusiasm, which always helps make an idea interesting. In the main, the essay has unity, continuity, and emphasis—all deriving from its form. It is the form that provides the structure both for the original one-paragraph essay and for the expanded five-paragraph paper.

Shaping the Essay

Remember first of all that a longer paper has essentially the same structure as a one-paragraph paper. Each has a beginning, a middle, and an end. Look at the essay on pages 135–36 and note the labels we have added. The first paragraph is the beginning; the second, third, and fourth paragraphs all belong to the middle or body of the paper; and the fifth paragraph is the end. To help you see this more clearly we'll put a skeleton of the five-paragraph paper into the familiar I-shape in which we first placed the student's one-paragraph paper. Thus, we have the following diagram:

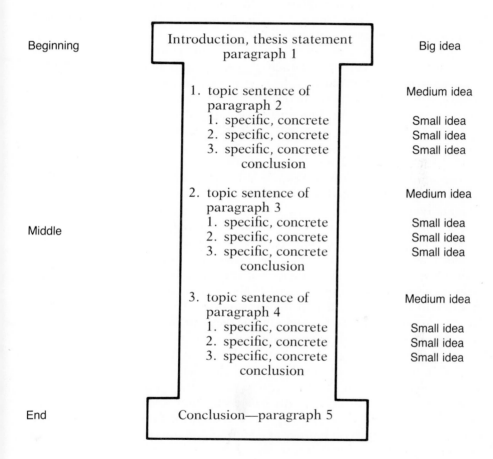

Beginning	Introduction, thesis statement paragraph 1	Big idea
	1. topic sentence of paragraph 2	Medium idea
	1. specific, concrete	Small idea
	2. specific, concrete	Small idea
	3. specific, concrete	Small idea
	conclusion	
	2. topic sentence of paragraph 3	Medium idea
Middle	1. specific, concrete	Small idea
	2. specific, concrete	Small idea
	3. specific, concrete	Small idea
	conclusion	
	3. topic sentence of paragraph 4	Medium idea
	1. specific, concrete	Small idea
	2. specific, concrete	Small idea
	3. specific, concrete	Small idea
	conclusion	
End	Conclusion—paragraph 5	

Now what we have done is put the opening paragraph in the crossbar at the top of the I. This first paragraph serves as the introduction to the paper, but at the same time it also contains the main idea of the whole paper, and because of this we call it, the *thesis statement*—that is, the statement that contains the controlling idea of the entire paper. (Remember, in your one-paragraph papers the topic sentence held the controlling idea.)

Next, we put the student's second, third, and fourth paragraphs in the column of the I, the narrow part. These three paragraphs develop the paper's thesis just as the small ideas in a one-paragraph paper develop its topic sentence, and in both cases they make up the middle part or body of the paper. Keep in mind that each of these three middle paragraphs is shaped exactly like the entire paragraph of a one-paragraph paper. Remember also that each one has a topic sentence with its main idea stated at the top or beginning of the paragraph. Additionally, each has three (more or less) small ideas, which we show on the diagram as "specific, concrete." (Actually, in the student's essay, every paragraph but one has its own conclusion at the bottom. Which one does not? How does the lack of a conclusion weaken the paragraph?)

There is, however, one very simple but important difference. The big idea in the topic sentence of each of these middle paragraphs is the big idea only in its own paragraph. It is not the biggest idea of the whole paper; it has now become subordinate to the big idea in the thesis statement in the first or introductory paragraph. Because it is smaller than the thesis-statement big idea but larger than the smaller, supporting ideas in its own paragraph, we call it a *medium idea*. This should be clear to you if you study the diagram on page 137.

The small ideas in the one-paragraph paper have moved up to become the topic sentences (medium ideas) of the three middle paragraphs, while the big idea of the topic sentence of the one-paragraph paper has become the big idea or thesis statement of the whole paper. This new form, the five-paragraph paper, is what we call the *one-three-nine* form.

One stands for the big idea in the thesis; *three* stands for the three medium ideas in the topic sentences of the three middle paragraphs; and *nine* stands for the total number of the specific and concrete, or small, ideas that we have in each of the three middle paragraphs. It might help us to understand the relations among these thirteen ideas and to grasp the significance of their various functions in contributing to the sense and form of the entire essay if we think of them as a family unit. Think of the *one* as a grandfather, of the *three* as his three children, of the *nine* as the three children of each of the first children—grandchildren of the old man. The first three children are equal to each other and subordinate to, or smaller than, their parent, though directly related to him. The grandchildren are all equal to each other and subordinate to, or smaller than, their respective parents; although directly related to their parents, they are only indirectly related to their grandfather. Keep in mind that of the thirteen, Grandfather is boss; he was the original big idea, and without his existence, none of the other twelve would have come into being. A similar relationship exists among the big, the medium, and the small ideas in our five-paragraph paper.

To help you get a mental image of the overall shape of a five-paragraph paper as well as of the individual paragraphs within it, especially the middle ones, we will draw an outline of the five paragraphs inside the form of the entire essay.

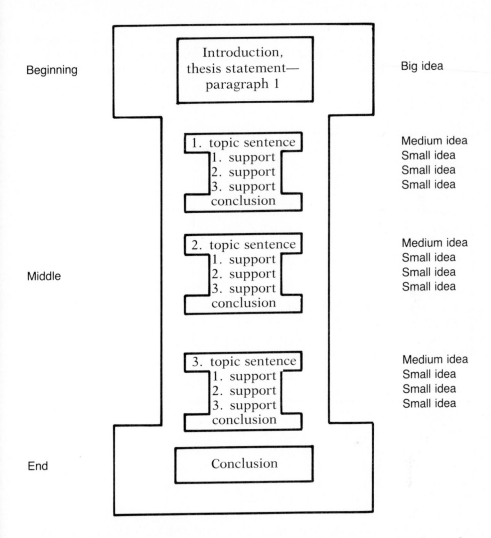

The next step is to examine the forms of the individual paragraphs in the student's essay. The first paragraph is diagramed below.

Both the first and the last paragraphs are in the shape of plain rectangles to suggest openness and a variety of possible shapes. We are not much concerned here with beginnings and endings for their own sakes. In the "beginning" paragraph, we recommend that your thesis statement be at the end with introductory material preceding it, for two reasons. First, you need some sort of background material to lead your reader up to the thesis statement—to show how you got there, as in the following introductory paragraph. You need somehow to generate interest in what you are going to be writing about. Second, placed at the bottom of your opening paragraph, the thesis statement is followed by the topic sentence of your first middle paragraph, which begins the development of the thesis. Conclusions you are already familiar with. Writing a conclusion for a five-paragraph paper is essentially the same as writing one for a one-paragraph paper. In concluding the one-paragraph paper you sum up less important ideas contained in the body of the paragraph; in concluding the longer paper you sum up the medium ideas, which are expressed in the topic sentences of each of your middle paragraphs.

I agree with Dan Wakefield in his standing up for sports in his essay "In Defense of the Fullback." However, I find myself opposed to his main idea that nothing we experience later on in life can compare in importance with our sports experiences in school. The expression used in describing the so-called glory was the fullback's "eighty-yard run," and the author makes it stand for the highest achievement in the athlete's life. Supposedly, the athlete will never again do anything else so great, and thus the rest of life will seem very dull. I <u>feel that just the normal living of life contains many experiences far greater than that</u> of the "eighty-yard run."	Beginning
	Big idea or thesis statement

Because all the middle paragraphs have the same shape and labels, we will diagram and discuss only the first middle paragraph of the student's paper. Remember that what we say about the first middle paragraph applies to all middle paragraphs in our system. A diagram of paragraph 2 from "In Defense of Life" appears on page 141.

Read paragraph 2 carefully. Notice how, by the simple act of diagramming the paragraph and by labeling its components, its faults and weaknesses are brought out into the open. You undoubtedly have many more ideas for improving this paragraph now than you did after reading it as it appeared in the essay. Is *marriage* the best word to use in the topic sentence? Should it, perhaps, be changed to *marriage and family life*, or *marriage and children*? Is the space devoted to the three small ideas uneven? Should the third small idea be lifted out of the Tad Jones sentence and be given more development and support by more specific illustrations of children's accomplishments? Or is the whole idea of children large enough to be made into a separate paragraph, distinct from the idea of marriage?

Or, within the scope of the paragraph as written—except for enlarging further on the idea of children's accomplishments—is there a possibility of slightly altering the Tad Jones sentence and using it as a part of the concluding sentence (the summing up)?

One of the greatest of all experiences of life is marriage.

BEGINNING
Medium idea or
topic sentence

Here young people are tested in ways and to degrees that they would never encounter in a football or basketball game. If a husband and wife are really in love with each other, they'll have a unity and teamwork superior to any squad's. The loyalty between husband and wife is based on a closer human relationship than the loyalty one team member owes to the other members. Raising children also brings with it experiences of all types. Looking at the children and knowing they are yours and that you must take care of them and raise them is a lot more challenging—and should be more satisfying—than four years of looking at the other members of the team on the field and around the campus. Many look at this time when their children are young and completely dependent on them as the most cherished period of their lives. When Tad Jones (the Yale coach quoted in Wakefield's essay) made the statement that the "big game was the most important moment in a player's life," he must have been forgetting the pride a parent feels when he sees his son or daughter graduate from college or when he admires a portrait of his family.

Small idea 1:
love between
husband and
wife

Small idea 2:
joys of
parenthood

MIDDLE

Small idea 3:
joys in children's accomplishments

Certainly, experiencing marriage and family is at least as thrilling as playing in the "big game."

Conclusion
END

One-three-nine. It's a strong, tightly knit form, and we think it will improve your writing. You have undoubtedly begun to wonder, however, if every essay must be exactly one-three-nine and why use one-three-nine in the first place. In answer to your first question: certainly not. An essay can have any number of paragraphs it needs to make its point. It will have, however, only one thesis, just as your school has only one president. But the number of middle paragraphs may vary from essay to essay. A short essay (any essay under roughly 1,000 words) may have two, three, four, or maybe even five middle paragraphs, depending on the paper's length and complexity. Each of these middle paragraphs may have two, three, four, five, or more small ideas supported by dozens of smaller ideas. In answer to the second question: we chose three and nine mainly because a 500- or 600-word paper usually requires about three medium ideas to support the thesis and three smaller ideas to support each medium idea. As a matter of fact, the number three turns up so often in so many quantitative, spatial, and logical relations that many people have attributed to it religious, mystical, and even magical properties. We don't need to believe in magic, however, to see that usually three reasons, three examples, or three illustrations will provide more support than two—although often two will suffice. On the other hand, it is usually superfluous to cite more than three examples or illustrations to support a single unified idea. Three is usually just about right. Consider, however, the one-three-nine relationship as only a suggestion for the structure of your paper, and don't be afraid to vary the three and the nine to suit your needs in a given paper. The one-three-nine form is meant to give you a sense of proportion in the structure of your paper, not to straitjacket you.

SUMMARY

1. The need for the multiparagraph paper arises when our main idea has several related but parallel and equal parts that can be classified under one large topic.
2. Attempting to impose form on a smaller, one-paragraph paper or trying to organize what are often at first only a few tentative ideas helps us structure the larger paper. In our search for form we focus on finite, specific concepts—something definite enough for our minds to "see" and begin thinking about. This process releases a stream of thought with a sufficient quantity of ideas to make up a larger paper; this is what an Anglo-Saxon poet called "unlocking the word hoard."
3. For our purposes, we have assumed the multiparagraph paper to be an essay of about five paragraphs. The first paragraph is an introduction containing a thesis usually placed at or close to the end of the paragraph. The second, third, and fourth paragraphs make up the middle part, or body, of the essay. They develop the thesis. The main idea in each of the middle paragraphs is in the topic sentence, located at the beginning of the paragraph. Since these main ideas are smaller than the big idea controlling the entire paper, yet larger than the small ideas beneath them, we call these ideas *medium* ideas. The fifth paragraph is the conclusion, in which we sum up the middle ideas and restate the thesis.
4. The overall shape of the five-paragraph paper is an I, the same shape

as the one-paragraph paper. The three middle paragraphs also have this shape; they are simply smaller versions of it. The introductory and concluding paragraphs have a rectangular shape to suggest the relative *width* or the general nature of the ideas contained in them as compared with the width of those in the middle paragraph.

5. *One-three* is an arithmetical description of the one-paragraph paper. *One-three-nine* describes the five-paragraph paper.

EXERCISE 42   *Analyze the middle paragraph outlined in the diagram on page 141 in light of the questions asked above it. Rewrite the paragraph, incorporating the suggestions below.*

1. Improve the wording of the big idea to make it correspond more closely to the paragraph's development.
2. Develop the second and third small ideas in more detail to give them emphasis equal to that given the first small idea.
3. Eliminate some of the generalizations in the development of the first small idea and replace them with more specific, concrete details for examples and illustrations.
4. Make the Tad Jones statement part of the conclusion and improve the existing concluding statement.

EXERCISE 43   *Diagram the third middle paragraph on page 136 according to the one-three-nine form. After you have done this, study it carefully; then rewrite it, making whatever alterations are necessary to improve it.*

EXERCISE 44   *Expand your one-paragraph paper on Olaf Torgerson (see Exercise 39, p. 120) into a one-three-nine essay, containing about 500 or 600 words in five paragraphs—the introduction or beginning rectangular, the three middle paragraphs I-shaped, and the fifth and final (conclusion or ending) rectangular. Consult the diagrams and explanations in Chapter 6 and 7, as well as the discussion of development in earlier chapters. This exercise will test what you have learned about writing.*

EXERCISE 45   *Write a one-three-nine paper of at least 600 words on the subject of life's satisfactions. This is partly the topic of the essay "In Defense of Life"; but we are not asking you to take that student's point of view or to defend any of his arguments. Parts of his essay may help to bring your own feelings and thoughts to the surface, but your essay should discuss the aspects of life that you believe are the most worthwhile for you and that give you the greatest satisfaction. The subject of a paper is not the same thing as the big idea. It is a larger, more general concept from which we derive*

*the thesis statement and big idea. As you can see from the ex-
amples below, the thesis statement and the big idea are distinct
from, although related to, the subject. The thesis statement is more
limited in scope than the subject of the paper; the big idea is the
most important part of the thesis statement: it is the part that will
be developed in the rest of the paper. In the first example, the big
idea is satisfactions that come from relations with other people.
The writer's job is to show in what ways these relations are satisfying. In the second example, the big idea is the writer's satisfying curiosity about the future. The last sentence of this example
is an example of a transitional sentence: it suggests the direction
that the rest of the paper is going to take.*

Example   *Subject*   Satisfactions in life.
Thesis statement   "As for me, my main satisfaction in life comes
from my relations with the people around me at home, at
school, and at work."

Example   *Subject*   Satisfactions in life.
Thesis statement   "One of my main pleasures in life is satisfying my curiosity about the future—my own future, the futures of members of my family and of friends, the future of the
world. For me, the unfolding of these futures is like watching
a movie or reading a book."

Example   *Subject*   Satisfactions in life.
Thesis statement   "My most satisfying experiences in life take
the form of various kinds of physical activity."

EXERCISE 46   *Write a one-three-nine paper of about 500 or 600 words describing the three main steps in a process such as making a dress,
tuning up an automobile engine, building a cabin, getting good
grades in college, or making a pair of sandals.*

EXERCISE 47   *Make another visit to Olaf Torgerson's family and describe a project the family has completed or an adventure they have shared.
Show how each of the three children makes a unique contribution
to the experience through some inherent or learned quality received from Olaf.*

Seeing the Paragraph Structure of the Essay

Below is an article by the tennis player and author Arthur Ashe, as it appeared in the *San Francisco Chronicle* in 1977. Ashe, who is 41 years old,

won the first United States Open Tennis championship, as an amateur in 1968, and the 1975 Wimbledon title.

BLACK YOUTH: PROSE INSTEAD OF PROS

Since my sophomore year at UCLA, I have become convinced that we blacks spend too much time on the playing fields and too little time in the libraries.

Please don't think of this attitude as being pretentious just because I am a black, single, professional athlete.

I don't have children, but I can make observations. I strongly believe that black culture spends too much time, energy, and effort raising, praising and teasing our black children about the dubious glories of professional sport.

All children need models to emulate—parents, relatives or friends. But when the child starts school, the influence of the parent is shared by teachers and classmates, by the lure of books, movies, ministers and newspapers, but most of all by television.

Which televised events have the greatest number of viewers? Sports—the Olympics, Super Bowl, Masters, World Series, pro basketball play-offs, Forest Hills, ABC-TV even has sports on Monday night prime time from April to December.

So your child gets a massive dose of O. J. Simpson, Kareem Abdul-Jabbar, Muhammad Ali, Reggie Jackson, Dr. J., Lee Elder and other pro athletes. And it is only natural that your child will dream of being a pro athlete himself.

But consider these facts: for the major professional sports of hockey, football, basketball, baseball, golf, tennis, and boxing, there are roughly only 3,170 major-league positions available (attributing 200 positions to golf, 200 to tennis, and 100 to boxing). And the annual turnover is small.

We blacks are a subculture of about 28 million. Of the 13.5 million men, 5 to 6 million are under 20 years of age, so your son has less than one chance in 1,000 of becoming a pro. Less than one in a thousand. Would you bet your son's future on something with odds of 999 to 1 against you? I wouldn't.

Unless a child is exceptionally gifted, you should know by the time he enters high school whether he has a future as an athlete. But what is more important is what happens if he doesn't graduate or doesn't receive a college scholarship or doesn't have an alternative job career. Our high-school dropout rate is several times the national average, which contributes to our unemployment rate of roughly twice the national average.

And how do you fight the figures in the newspapers every day? Ali has earned more than $30 million boxing, O. J. just signed for $2.5 million, Dr. J. for almost $3 million, Reggie Jackson for $2.8 million, Nate Archibald for $400,000 a year. All that money, recognition, attention, free cars, girls, jobs in the offseason—no wonder there is Pop Warner football, Little League baseball, National Junior Tennis League tennis, hockey practice at 5 A.M. and pickup basketball games in any center city at any hour.

There must be some way to assure that the 999 who try but don't make it to pro sports don't wind up on street corners or in unemployment lines.

Unfortunately, our most widely recognized role models are athletes and entertainers—"runnin'" and "jumpin'" and "singin'" and "dancin'."

While we are 60 percent of the National Basketball Association, we are less than four percent of the doctors and lawyers. While we are about 35 percent of major league baseball, we are less than two percent of the engineers. While we are about 40 percent of the National Football League, we are less than 11 percent of construction workers such as carpenters and bricklayers.

Our greatest heroes of the century have been athletes—Jack Johnson, Joe Louis, and Muhammad Ali. Racial and economic discrimination forced us to channel our energies into athletics and entertainment. These were the ways out of the ghetto, the ways to get that Cadillac, those regular shoes, that cashmere sport coat.

Somehow, parents must instill a desire for learning alongside the desire to be Walt Frazier. Why not start by sending black professional athletes into high schools to explain the facts of life?

I have often addressed high school audiences and my message is always the same. For every hour you spend on the athletic field, spend two in the library. Even if you make it as a pro athlete, your career will be over by the time you are 35. You will need that diploma.

Have these pro athletes explain what happens if you break a leg, get a sore arm, have one bad year or don't make the cut for five or six tournaments. Explain to them the star system, wherein for every O. J. earning millions there are six or seven others making $15,000 or $20,000, $30,000 a year.

But don't just have Walt Frazier or O. J. or Abdul-Jabbar address your class. Invite a benchwarmer or a guy who didn't make it. Ask him if he sleeps every night. Ask him whether he was graduated. Ask him what he would do if he became disabled tomorrow. Ask him where his old high-school athletic buddies are.

We have been on the same roads—sports and entertainment—too long. We need to pull over, fill up at the library, and speed away to Congress and the Supreme Court, the unions and business world. We need more Barbara Jordans, Andrew Youngs, union cardholders, Nikki Giovannis and Earl Graveses. Don't worry; we will still be able to sing and dance and run and jump better than anybody else.

I'll never forget how proud my grandmother was when I graduated from UCLA in 1966. Never mind the Davis Cup in 1968, 1969, and 1970. Never mind the Wimbledon title, Forest Hills, etc. To this day, she still doesn't know what those names mean.

What mattered to her was that of her more than 30 children and grandchildren, I was the first to be graduated from college, and a famous college at that. Somehow, that made up for all those floors she scrubbed all those years.

The message of Ashe's article is clear, but we are principally concerned here with the article's structure rather than its ideas. Although it is only approximately 800 words, it is divided into twenty paragraphs. This is especially interesting because we have been encouraging you to develop the habit of writing longer paragraphs, longer because they are generally more fully developed, more tightly organized and connected paragraphs. As we mentioned, "An Open Letter to Parents" was published in a newspaper, and paragraphs in newspaper articles are almost always shorter than those in books or in most magazine articles. This is partly because of such technical reasons as spatial arrangements on a sheet of newsprint and layout in the composing room, but also partly because of the psychology of the newspaper reader. Given the narrowness of a standard newspaper column, a paragraph of only 150 words (a common length of a good, middle paragraph in a student's theme) will look discouragingly long to a reader, since it is about four inches long. Newspaper readers are notoriously in a hurry, and long paragraphs (or paragraphs that *look* long) may easily turn them off. For that matter, long paragraphs in a book tend to discourage readers. Why do you think this is so? What is there about a page of solid lines of print, unrelieved by indentations, that makes us wince and tempts us to scan and skip? And why do indentations, on the other hand, suggest a breathing spell for the mind?

Let's imagine Ashe's article as an editorial to be published as an essay in a book and, taking some liberties with Ashe's work, let's see what happens if we rearrange the paragraphs.

Here are the first three paragraphs of the article rearranged as one paragraph:

> Since my sophomore year at UCLA, I have become convinced that we blacks spend too much time on the playing fields and too little time in the libraries. Please don't think of this attitude as being pretentious just because I am a black, single, professional athlete. I don't have children, but I can make observations. I strongly believe that black culture spends too much time, energy, and effort raising, praising, and teasing our black children about the dubious glories of professional sport.

Which sentence do you think contains the thesis statement? Do you see any other ways in which you could reconstruct these first three paragraphs for an introduction, making only minor changes in the wording?

EXERCISE 48   *Proceed now with the entire article and try logically and coherently, not arbitrarily, to reduce the remaining seventeen paragraphs to five or six or seven, making only a few technical changes in the wording. Don't be afraid, however, to shift whole phrases or entire sentences around if you think it would improve your beginnings, transitions, and conclusions of paragraphs and your rearrangement in general. You may use the first three paragraphs as we put them above, or reorganize an introduction any way you think works well and does not distort Ashe's meanings.*

Seed Thoughts in Ashe's Essay and Some Other Ideas

Any thoughtful piece of writing generates ideas in the reader's mind. Undoubtedly, thoughts and questions have arisen in your mind after working on Ashe's article and discussing it and other students' revisions of it in class. We might classify a few of these likely ideas as follows:

First, Ashe's article, for a number of reasons, was addressed to black people. This in itself raises questions. Although some of his reasons are obvious, others are perhaps not so obvious. What might some of these other reasons be? And why might Ashe's message be especially important to black parents and students? But, even as it stands, in what ways would it apply to other minority groups? How would you modify the article's contents were you to address it, say, to Puerto Ricans, Chicanos, Asiatics, Indians, or any other kind of minority in America? Then, again, doesn't much of what he says apply to whites or to anyone anywhere in our world?

Second, Ashe argues the value of a college education for blacks, but he also urges the importance of at least a high-school diploma. All over America, in every class and ethnic group, many people are expressing doubts about the validity of the high-school diploma. They argue that the diploma has no meaning anymore because it is no longer necessary to know much to get one. A certificate obtained by passing a state proficiency test, they say, is worth more because you have to know more than what high schools require for graduation to get it. They assert, also, that high-school, junior-high, and even grammar-school classes have become so disorderly that only the most highly motivated students learn anything. They contend that the less motivated students fall by the wayside and yet are passed on to the next grade whether or not they have learned anything, because nobody really cares about them. Then, too, they point out that you don't need the diploma to go on to college because some junior colleges will admit anyone eighteen or over, even without a high-school diploma. And, finally, they say that high-school teachers are either creeps or hippies, or too old and don't understand students, or that the good ones are fed up with discipline problems and have just given up, or don't care about any students except the smart, well-behaved ones. What do you think about these things?

Yet the public-school buildings are still there, the books are there, the teachers still sign in and out and go to class. And isn't the notion that public-school education can somehow be valuable still here in all of us, as it is in Ashe? What do you think about all these things? Or at least about some of them?

Third, the article supports book learning and libraries and especially college, but it restricts its discussion of the purpose of higher education as a means to either an economic or a social end or both. Nevertheless, most of us believe that, in addition to helping us get better jobs, achieve higher social positions, and make more money, there are other reasons for going to college. What do you think some of these other reasons are? Make a short list of the reasons you think Ashe's grandmother must have had for being so proud of her grandson when he graduated from UCLA. (You might want to use something from this list in the following exercise.)

EXERCISE 49   *Many thoughts and questions, then, come to us on reading Ashe's article. Your job is to take some thought or question from the article or from the ideas above, or from thoughts and questions of your own and develop a 500-word essay on the ideas you choose. Use one-three-nine as your basic structure. This does not mean you must have exactly three middle paragraphs or exactly three small ideas in each of the middle paragraphs. Use the number of middle paragraphs and the number of supporting ideas that best fits your thoughts. Try, however, not to spend too much time on your introduction and conclusion, neither of these paragraphs should be over 75 words.*

Methods of Paragraph Development

8

In Chapters 6 and 7 we examined the relationship between the ideas or thoughts of a piece of writing and its shape or architecture, first in the paragraph and then in the short essay. In general, most prose falls into one of two categories, because there are basically two types of things we want to say: either we want to tell about something that happened (narration), or we want to talk about our ideas and thoughts (exposition). When we tell about something that happened (that occupied physical space and moved through time) either to ourselves or to someone else, we are writing *narration*. Example:

> Harrison Hollowell drew his rusty 44 and fired at the yellow eyes shining in the dark. The gun went roota-to-toot. With an oath, his deadly enemy, Jake Fogarty, leaped over the garden wall and ran for his life down the dark alley. Overhead the wind moaned in the trees. Harrison Hollowell, cool-like, walked around the end of the block to head him off at the intersection.

> Father got all of us out of the sack at 4:30 A.M., and we climbed into the family jalopy and headed for L.A.

> "Veni, vidi, vici." (I came, I saw, I conquered.)
> —Julius Caesar

Most of your writing in school will be exposition—papers, essay examinations, and themes. You are writing *exposition* when you expound, explain, or show your thoughts and ideas and facts about a subject. For example:

150

To the eternal glory of this world we are the oblong people, and we believe that everything and everyone else should be oblong. I personally think that anyone who disagrees with us should be whipped, drawn and quartered, and roasted over a slow fire. To be oblong and to believe in the glory of oblongness must be right or we would not be oblong and think oblong. Hail oblong!

I like apple pie better than berry pie because apple pie doesn't have any seeds to get stuck between my teeth.

"I care not what course others may take. But as for me, give me liberty or give me death."

—Patrick Henry

Remember, narration tells about something that happened—something that actually happened (nonfiction) or something made up (fiction, a story); and exposition expresses your thoughts and ideas. Writing often contains both narration and exposition. Many paragraphs use still other types of development. In this chapter, we will discuss six methods of developing paragraphs according to the way in which we want to say something: classification, definition, comparison-contrast, comparison-contrast/definition, process, and description.

Although there are many methods of rhetorical development of paragraphs, we think these six are the most basic. And, once again, we believe that learning a method for saying something will help you learn to say it on paper, first, by helping you to think and second, by helping you to organize your thinking.

Classification

As you remember from our discussion in Chapter 5, classification is the process by which large bodies of information are divided into smaller related groups on the basis of some principle of categorizing. The following student paragraph illustrates the concept of classification as it pertains to paragraph development.

> While most people are content to enjoy members of the cat family as domestic pets or to view them in zoos, scientists who study them have found it useful to classify the world's felines into such zoological categories as *Felis*, *Panthera*, *Lynx*, and *Acinonyx*. One division, *Felis*, is based largely upon the refined development of a small group of hyoid bones at the base of the tongue, which allows these carnivores to purr and to express themselves by mewing or screaming; they cannot roar. Their pupils are usually vertical, and they have retractable claws. *Felis* includes the mountain lion and the domestic cat. Among the larger cats of the division *Panthera*—lions, tigers, leopards, jaguars—the hyoid bones of the tongue do not develop as they do in the

smaller cats. As a result the bigger cats cannot purr, and they express themselves by roaring or coughing. *Lynx* includes the Canada Lynx and the bay Lynx, which differ from members of the other two divisions in possessing short tails, large tufted ears, and twenty-eight instead of thirty teeth. The cheetah, or hunting leopard, has characteristics that make it difficult to classify among the other members of the cat family. The cheetah has a normal hyoid but has greatly elongated legs and nonretractable claws. It cannot climb, and it possesses certain doglike characteristics. Accordingly, it is placed alone in the division *Acinonyx*. These divisions—based on biological observations, are part of the science of classification called *taxonomy*, which provides scientists with a means of categorizing and preserving vast amounts of information.

In this classification paragraph, the student has a little essay complete in itself. Often, however, the need for developing a paragraph by classification arises in a multiparagraph essay. For example, you might be writing about why you approve (or disapprove) of the federal government's paying members of the armed forces for taking college courses. Regardless of how you stand on the question, to clarify your discussion you would have to classify the various kinds of government programs or the different ways of qualifying for eligibility for these benefits.

The following paragraph, from chapter twenty-four in Will Durant's *The Age of Faith*, classifies the kinds of battles the European peasants of the Middle Ages fought against nature.

While their masters fought one another, the peasants of Europe fought the greater battle, more heroic and unsung, of man against nature. Between the eleventh and the thirteenth century the sea had thirty-five times swept over barriers and across the Lowlands, creating new gulfs and bays where once there had been land, and drowning 100,000 persons in a century. From the eleventh to the fourteenth century the peasants of these regions, under their princes and abbots, transported blocks of stone from Scandinavia and Germany, and built the "Golden Wall" behind which the Belgians and the Dutch have developed two of the most civilized states in history. Thousands of acres were rescued from the sea, and by the thirteenth century the Lowlands were latticed with canals. From 1179 to 1257 the Italians cut the famous Naviglio Grande, or Great Canal, between Lake Maggiore and the Po, fertilizing 86,485 acres of land. Between the Elbe and the Oder patient immigrants from Flanders, Frisia, Saxony, and the Rhineland turned the marshy Mooren into rich fields. The superabundant forests of France were progressively cleared, and became the farms that through centuries of political turmoil have kept France fed. Perhaps it was this mass heroism of *clearance, drainage, irrigation*, and *cultivation* [italics mine], rather than any victories of war or trade, that provided the foundation on which, in final analysis, rest all triumphs of European civilization in the last 700 years.

The paragraph's organization is a simple I-beam. The first sentence is the topic sentence and states the main argument of the paragraph. The next sentence launches the detail of the body of the paragraph. The concluding sentence names the four different classes or types of war that the peasants fought against nature and restates, though in different words, the main idea or argument of the topic sentence.

EXERCISE 50   *Write a classification paragraph by answering one of the following questions, or one you make up yourself. Give a brief explanation or description of each type or class and give an example of two of each.*

1. How many basic kinds of love are there, or of lovers?
2. What are the basic types of professional boxers (not weight classes)?
3. What are the basic types of recreational vehicles?
4. What are the basic types of running backs in football—or linebackers, or guards, quarterbacks, and so on?
5. What are the basic types of rock music—or any other kind of music, or concerts?
6. What are the basic types of movies?
7. What are the basic types of students, or teachers?

EXERCISE 51   *Write a classification paragraph by answering one of the following questions and arguing that one of the ways or classes is superior to the others or that you prefer it to the others. Or make up a subject of your own.*

1. How many basic ways are there for getting a person to say yes?
2. How many basic types of marriage ceremonies are there?
3. How many ways are there for cooking steaks, or anything else?
4. How many basic ways are there for using tobacco?
5. What are the basic ways to get money?
6. How many basic ways are there to goof off?
7. What are the basic ways to get yourself liked or disliked?
8. What are the basic ways to make yourself the life of the party, or to rain on someone else's parade?
9. What are the basic ways for obtaining knowledge or learning?

Definition

Often, in order to clarify our thoughts for ourselves and to clarify our meaning for a reader, we need first to define something—a word, a term, or a type, or a quality. Sometimes a dictionary definition is not enough, for we need to explain or define the particular way in which we are using the word or term. Our definition may be a one-paragraph paper, complete in itself, or it may be a single paragraph of a multiparagraph paper.

The following student paragraph attempts to define a term that almost defies definition. But the term is widely used (and often leads to confusion), so such an attempt is worth making. The writer simplifies the job by reducing the term to, and dealing with, what to him is the term's most significant application.

It is almost impossible to define precisely the term *ethnic group* as it is used in our society. Perhaps the task would be simpler if the term were divided into two parts. There is, first, the "voluntary" ethnic group, comprising groups of Scots, Irish, Poles, Swedes, Germans, Hungarians, and the like, who get together for sports events, dances, weddings, beer drinking, wine tasting—perhaps wearing ethnic clothing and eating ethnic foods—in order to preserve customs and traditions. It is the group's own choice to cultivate its ethnicity, its degree of separateness. Ethnic affiliation is not imposed on these groups. The other division is the "involuntary" ethnic group. This group has had its ethnicity perpetuated, its isolation and separateness imposed on it, by a dominant group or dominating majority. Assimilation is the key to understanding the distance between the voluntary and involuntary groups. Most people, either as individuals or as groups, want to be assimilated into the whole. They do not want to be separate; they want to belong. The most decisive factor in recent ethnic assimilation in America has been skin color. We might, then, define an involuntary ethnic group in the U.S. as any group of people whose skin color reveals the area of their origins to be Asia, Africa, the South Pacific, or the western hemisphere south of the Rio Grande.

The following paragraph is from Eric Hoffer's essay "The Role of the Undesirables." As we see in the first sentence, it is not the word *pioneer* but rather the *people who became pioneers* that Hoffer is going to define.

(1) Who were the pioneers? (2) Who were the men who left their homes and went into the wilderness? (3) A man rarely leaves a soft spot and goes deliberately in search of hardship and privation. (4) People become attached to the places they live in; they drive roots. (5) A change of habitat is a painful act of uprooting. (6) A man who has made good and has a standing in his community stays put. (7) The successful businessmen, farmers, and workers usually stayed where they were. (8) Who then left for the wilderness and the unknown? (9) Obviously those who had not made good; men who went broke and never amounted to much; men who though possessed of abilities were too impulsive to stand the daily grind; men who were slaves of their appetites—drunkards, gamblers, and woman-chasers; outcasts—fugitives from justice and ex-jailbirds. (10) There were no doubt some who went in search of health—men suffering with TB, asthma, heart trouble. (11) Finally there was a sprinkling of young and middle-aged in search of adventure.

Starting with a question is often an effective way to begin a paragraph of definition. The second sentence, although another question, begins defining the pioneer type: it is restricted to those who leave home for the wilderness. Then the next five sentences, almost half of the paragraph, attack the problem from the rear by defining the people who did *not* become pioneers. This is an especially effective approach because it stimulates the readers's imagination and creates suspense about the positive definition to come. The last half of the paragraph gives the opposite counterparts of the nonpioneers and further defines the person who does become a pioneer.

EXERCISE 52   *Write two one-paragraph definition papers on two subjects of your own choosing, or on two from the following list. In the first paper, use the style of the student's paragraph. In the second, tell what your subject isn't as well as what it is, roughly, in Hoffer's style.*

1. Define some sort of ideal: a human being; a quality such as love, courage, friendship; a husband or a wife; a job applicant; a party; a vacation; a house or home; a college; a teacher or a student; transportation; a trip; or whatever.
2. Define an *active member* of the Third World in a college.
3. Define the successful professional athlete. Define his or her athletic abilities and traits of character and personality. Don't give names of athletes or merely define the term professional.
4. Define families whose income is below the poverty level.
5. Define in Hoffer's style one of the following: rednecks, hard hats, Archie Bunkers, junkies, republicans, democrats, liberals, hawks, doves, or whatever.

The following paragraph is from *Pursuit of Understanding: Autobiography of an Education*, by Esther Cloudman Dunn. In the preceding paragraph in her book, Dunn likened teachers to artists but pointed out the differences between the human material the teacher works with and the inert material of marble, canvas, or music paper that a sculptor, painter, and composer work with.

> For the teacher there is no such passive, receptive material [that is, the material artists work with]. The thing upon which he [the teacher] has to impress his concept is a human being. This is restless material, with a will and direction of its own: ways of study, tricks of thinking; things slowly and mysteriously built up hour by hour since the moment of birth. These already give character and bent to the mind and imagination of the being who is to be taught. These positive qualities have their good side. The ways of thinking and feeling in a pupil are sometimes gifted, promising good and even great powers for his future. They often surpass the mental equipment of the teacher.

EXERCISE 53   *Write a paragraph answering the following questions:*

1. Do you think Dunn's paragraph is definition? Why or why not?
2. If you think it is definition, what is she defining?

Comparison-Contrast

In a comparison-contrast paragraph two arguments or sets of facts, or things, or persons are set up side by side and explained or described by showing their differences or their similarities and differences, as in the following paragraph.

A human heart and an automobile fuel pump share a number of similarities as well as differences. First, both are reciprocating, positive displacement pumps. Both have inlet and discharge check valves to open up for inflow and outflow and to prevent backflow. Both are starkly simple in function: the human heart's purpose is to pump enough blood for the body's needs; the fuel pump must pump enough fuel for the automobile's needs. Both pumps are crucial in determining the performance of the entire system of which they are parts. But within this framework of mechanical analogy there are striking differences. The human heart, composed of living tissue, is an engine in itself. The fuel pump, composed of metal and perhaps synthetic material for its diaphragm, is a lifeless mechanical slave; it is not in itself an engine. Through the motions of cams or gears or electrical current it must be moved by the engine it serves. But the heart, day in and day out, year upon year, like any other internal combustion engine and like the greater engine it serves, pulsates back and forth, contracting and expanding on its own volition, consuming the fuel and the oxygen to make it work, regulating its speed to conform to its body's needs, tirelessly responding to the curious little tissue deep within it called the *pacemaker*. Indeed, the word *heart* conjures up the notion of such preemptive power and necessity, such patient and almost princely dedication to its purpose, that we use the word figuratively to describe any part of something that is central and crucial to its whole (*heartland* of a nation, *heart* of the matter, "Big Two-*Hearted* River," good-*hearted*). It is, of course, interesting—for many of us, even gratifying— to find mysteries in the human heart where we cannot find them in the fuel pump of a Dodge Dart. It is, however, noteworthy that lately medical science and medical engineering have linked the heart much more closely to all strictly mechanical things—simply by rendering it stoppable, startable, and repairable.

Comparison-contrast is an excellent form in which to state an argument. Since it can lodge both sides of the argument (pro and con) under the same roof, it allows the writer to show readers the gap between what has commonly passed for truth and what the writer sees as the *real* truth about a subject. In the following student paragraph, the writer tries to dispel some popular misconceptions about a renowned Marine fighter squadron of the Second World War known as the "Black Sheep."

According to Frank E. Walton, the NBC-TV program about the famed "Pappy" Boyington and his Black Sheep Squadron is filled with distortions and misconceptions. (**I.**) Perhaps its main distortion characterizes the flyers as immature and rowdy. (**A.**) They are depicted as 18- and 19-year-olds who get into fistfights and occasionally run off with some other squadron's supplies. (B.) Such was not the case, explains Walton. (C.) The average age of the Black Sheep was nearly 24, and there were twelve pilots 26 or older, including three in their thirties, none of whom was ever seen fistfighting or "borrowing" from other units. (**II.**) NBC presents the pilots as congenital misfits, people who would have little chance of succeeding outside the military. (A.) In a TV talk show, series star Robert Conrad supported such an image when he remarked that "they had failed at everything they'd ever done. None of them could make it on his own." (B.) Walton counters this charge by pointing out that of the Black Sheep who returned to civilian life, seven became owners or presidents of business firms, two became mayors of cities, three lawyers, one a professor, and one a stockbroker. (**III.**) Perhaps the most damaging implication came from "Pappy" Boyington himself, who was the series' technical director. (A.) Said Boyington in an interview appearing in the Los Angeles *Herald Examiner*, "They had nothing to lose. . . . They knew if they distinguished themselves, they might get easier sentences." (B.) Walton takes issue with Boyington's statement by asserting that no member of the squadron was up for disciplinary action and, further, that not one Black Sheep *ever* faced disciplinary action during the time the squadron was operating in the Pacific. (Conclusion.) Concludes Walton, who was the squadron's intelligence officer, "It is ironic that the Hollywood "showbiz" technique . . . should have twisted what is one of the great performances of the war into such an inept travesty. The dramatization of the real facts about the Black Sheep's performance could be a high adventure story of which we could all be proud."

Notice that the approach of using primary and secondary support lends itself well to the comparison-contrast structure. The roman numeral categories each take up a point of contention. The A category under the roman numeral I presents the fabricated Hollywood image of the Black Sheep, while B and C present Walton's refutations. In placing the image and the refutation side by side in each instance, the writer never lets the reader forget which part of the subject is being argued. Such close juxtapositioning of the pros and cons probably makes for the most effective presentation of comparison-contrast, especially for the development of an argument.

Often, too, comparison-contrast works well in developing description. In the following paragraph from Moritz Thomsen's *Living Poor*, the first half deals with Ramon, except for the opening or topic sentence, and the second half is concerned mainly with Orestes. But even though the two descriptions are relatively separate in the paragraph, they are still each close enough to the other to clarify each other by comparison-contrast.

(1) It was amazing to compare the faces of the two brothers, faces which were almost identical in their features, and find such disparate qualities. (2) Ramon's face was all delight, quickness, light. (3) His humor was constant and a real part of his way of seeing things; life was a great joke in spite of everything. (4) He was like a trick pony, quick on his legs, volatile, a real

prancer. (5) Orestes was a work horse. (6) There wasn't a trick in him; he was built for the long pull. (7) His sense of humor, unlike Ramon's, which was a bubbling over of youth and optimism (and many times quite foolish), was black, bitter, and profound. (8) Everyone in town laughed with Ramon, he was so quick and lightly mocking. (9) But no one laughed when Orestes spoke. (10) His humor was much deeper and cutting. (11) A couple of months after we built the chicken coops, when Orestes realized that I thought his jokes were something quite special, he began to like me. (12) It was always hard to tell with Orestes, but it's almost impossible to dislike someone who thinks your jokes are bellybusters.

In the second sentence Thomsen specifically describes the expression and play of light in Ramon's face, but nowhere in the paragraph does he describe Orestes'. It isn't necessary, because we can imagine that, by contrast, Orestes' face would be serious, somber, or perhaps gloomy or satiric. Note, also, that although the last half is mainly about Orestes, the subordinate part of sentence seven and all of sentence eight, about Ramon, help to tie the comparisons together, by keeping both Ramon and Orestes in our minds at the same time.

The beauty of comparison-contrast is that, in the first place, it gives the writer a ready-made method that is easy to follow and, in the second place, it lends itself well to almost any sort of idea development because the appearance or nature of almost any single thing is sharpened when it is placed alongside its opposite or reverse. Most people, for example, have been fascinated by the fact that in the United States the lowest and the highest spots in the country (except in Alaska), Death Valley and Mount Whitney, are only a few miles apart. They render each other more impressive by their contrasting proximity.

Consider Eric Hoffer's paragraph defining the pioneers: could it just as properly be called a comparison-contrast paragraph as a definition paragraph? Does the part devoted to the nonpioneer type make the pioneer type, by contrast, stand out in sharper relief than it otherwise would? And how does the comparison-contrast enrich the paragraph by suggesting further ideas, although unspoken, about American society?

EXERCISE 54   *Select one of the following subjects or one of your own choice to write a paragraph using comparison-contrast to develop an argument. Use pairs of pro and con statements in the same sentence or in adjoining sentences, similar to the method used in the paragraph on the Black Sheep.*

1. Compare and contrast two cars—one American, the other foreign—in about the same price range or of comparable popularity.
2. Compare and contrast some subject of which you have close knowledge and about which hearsay or popular belief are contrary to the facts as you know them (see the Black Sheep paragraph), for example:
   a. popular notions about the high cost of athletic programs (or some

particular sport such as football or basketball) to the school (high school or college) and the truth as you know it or

b. popular ideas about nutrition and the facts about it as you know them

c. popular ideas about the harmfulness of marijuana and your notion of the truth—or vice versa

d. hearsay or gossip about a person and the truth about him or her

e. some stereotype such as the belief that bad people are interesting and good people are dull

EXERCISE 55   *Write a paragraph that compares-contrasts one of the following subjects. You do not have to argue that one of them is superior to the other; simply explain, define, or describe them by comparison-contrast, roughly in the style of the paragraph from* Living Poor.

1. The social needs and problems of high-school girls and high-school boys.
2. The home environments of an oldest child and a youngest child in the same family.
3. Surfers and high-school athletes.
4. Some aspect of Latin culture and Anglo culture.
5. The mountains and the beach or seashore.
6. Professional and college football.
7. College athletes and high-school athletes.
8. A good blind date and a bad one.

Comparison-Contrast Definition

A mixture of comparison-contrast and definition is often quite effective in developing a paragraph of argument.

In the following paragraph a student uses a writing assignment to disagree courteously with a remark his instructor had made about the white man's "monstrous" treatment of the Indians in America.

> I think that the white man treated the American Indian very badly, but not monstrously. First, as applied to men, the word monstrous, by definition, means abnormal or freakish, and therefore an unhuman kind of badness. According to what I have learned in history, the white man's treatment of the Indian was traditional and typical of the way any conquering groups treated a defeated native group. When the Aryans from the north conquered the native people of India around 1600 B.C., they enslaved the defeated population (who had a superior culture, by the way) and started the caste system, which imposed artificial inequalities on the conquered people. When the Romans defeated a foreign country, they usually gave the defeated people two choices—enslavement or death. (And this has affected European history up to the present.) The Anglo-Saxon people, when they conquered

England, apparently killed all the Celtic natives they could find, and the rest of the Celts fled to Wales and Scotland, and Cornwall, or across the sea to Ireland. (I understand that this is to blame for some of the sufferings of the Irish people today and for the poverty of some of the present populations of Scotland and Wales.) Therefore, I believe that the white man's behavior toward the American Indian was traditional and typical of human beings doing unjust, cruel, and terrible things but not typical of monsters. So we don't have to go to the nonhuman, abnormal monsters; the badness of human beings is bad enough, and the white man in America behaved with typically human, not monstrous, badness.

This is argumentive exposition developed by *definition, comparison-contrast*, examples from history, and logical arrangement of the material. The student quickly defines the key word whose use by his teacher he has disagreed with. Next, by appealing to the authority of history, he compares the white man's treatment of the American Indians with that of conquerors in the past, and gives three specific examples of such historic behavior. By logical argument, then, we must assume that because the white man's behavior was so similar to that of conquerors in other times and places, it is typical and relatively normal and therefore human rather than monstrous.

Well, neither the student's paragraph nor the teacher's remark is the final statement on the subject. Nevertheless, the student's paragraph is effective; he has forced the teacher to take the argument seriously and to reply in similar kind.

EXERCISE 56   *Do one of the following assignments.*

1. We often hear people say that the game of baseball is like a ballet. (Who publicly first said that?—Red Smith, William Saroyan, Paul Gallico, or someone else years before these men flourished?) If you are only a baseball player or fan, look up the word *ballet* in at least three dictionaries and encyclopedias, talk to people knowledgeable about ballet, see a live performance, if possible, or a least parts of a ballet in a movie or on TV. Then write a paragraph in which you agree or disagree with the statement that "baseball is like a ballet."

   Use the first-meaning definition from a dictionary to define the word *ballet*. Using that definition as your guide, develop your *pro* or *con* topic sentence by examples from ballet and baseball in which you compare and contrast the game with the art form to support your position.
2. Write a paragraph in which you define what you think is a successful person and compare-contrast him with an unsuccessful one.
3. Can a person be a good human being but unsuccessful? And vice versa? Write a paragraph in which you define an unsuccessful but good person and compare-contrast him with his opposite.

Process

In a process paragraph the writer tells the reader the process or procedure for making or doing something. A process paragraph is a paragraph of instructions, and the order of its development should be the orderly steps in which the process is to be carried out, or in which the thing is to be done or made. In the following paragraph, the student writer instructs the reader, by exposition, in the process to be followed in preparing to attend a rock concert.

HOW TO PREPARE FOR AN ALL DAY, OUTDOOR ROCK CONCERT

First, and most important, buy your tickets in advance. Discuss with your friends who is going and decide how many you will be. It is most important that you enjoy the company you are going with, and it is especially nice if you are going with a group of people. Perhaps within that group there is a member of the opposite sex to whom you are most attracted. This makes for an even more enjoyable time (I speak from experience). But if this is not possible, a pleasant time may still be had. Next, choose the mode of transportation. If you have a group. the sports car is out. Vans, station wagons, or VW buses are ideal. Once you have decided upon these major details, you can relax until the concert; but when the big day finally arrives, there are many other things to prepare. If the weather is hot, dress in something cool and comfortable, like jeans and a loose T-shirt. If you are the type who likes being high make sure you have the necessary items packed and ready to go. If you smoke cigarettes, make sure you have at least two packs on hand in case the cigarette machine is a mile away. As for food, there are two options—either pack your own (it can be a bit clumsy to carry) or buy it there (it can be costly, barely edible, and a hassle to get to). A few other items might include suntan lotion, if you burn easily; sunglasses, for sensitive eyes; a blanket, if you are lucky enough to be on the field; a camera, for remembrance; and perhaps a wide-brimmed hat, for those with sensitive scalps. Looking back I believe I've covered just about everything. Oh—one last thing—have a great time.

The next paragraph is from Helen Buckler's *Dr. Dan: Pioneer in American Surgery*, a biography of the famous black surgeon (who was also of American Indian descent), Daniel Hale Williams. Here Buckler tells us how Dr. Williams completed an historic operation he performed in Chicago, in July 1893. It is generally believed to be the first successful heart operation.

First he irrigated the wound with normal salt solution of 100 degrees Fahrenheit, which by that time was about room temperature. Then he grasped the edges of the pulsating wound with long smooth forceps. With not a little difficulty, he held the fluttering edges together and, using a continuous suture of fine catgut, he managed to close the wound. Next he closed the intercostal and sub-cartilaginous wounds, again using catgut. For the carti-lages and the skin, he changed to silkworm gut and left a few long sutures in the external stitches. They would permit easy removal in case infection or hermorrhage should develop, though he prayed it would not. Then he ap-plied a dry dressing, straightened his aching back, and mopped his brow. The silent, intent circle around him stirred; someone spoke. The historic op-eration was over.

The main difference between these two process paragraphs is that of tense or time. Buckler's paragraph tells about or narrates a process that was followed by the surgeon, a process that has already been completed, while the paragraph on preparing for a rock concert tells about a process for anyone to consider following in the future. Buckler's paragraph is narration, the student's paragraph is exposition.

EXERCISE 57   *Write a process paragraph of at least 250 words on one of the following subjects:*

1. How to give a party.
2. How to make a piece of pottery.
3. How to make a dress.
4. How to cook some sort of dish.
5. How to write an essay.
6. How to study for a midterm or final.
7. How to read a book.
8. How to paint a house, "thinwall' a sheetrock wall, tile a bathroom, or whatever.
9. How to meditate.
10. How to go trout fishing.
11. How to prepare for a camping trip, skiing trip, or whatever.
12. Or write about anything you know how to do or make.

Description

Most of us are too ready to dismiss something with a sweeping judgment such as "it was terrific"; it was a bummer"; "it was beautiful"; "it was a drag"; "it was boring, boring, boring"; "I couldn't stand it"; or "man, that was really something." These simplistic judgments get in our way. They prevent us from scrutinizing what we experience, from zeroing in on what really happened. The antidote for this habit is to look and listen carefully to what you experience and then describe the experience in-stead of leaping to judge it.

Although description is simply "telling it like it is," it is always your job to interpret the experience and thoughtfully select and describe what is significant, revealing, and interesting about it instead of vainly attempting to put down everything. The writers of the following paragraphs do not make many judgments. They simply guide readers through an arrangement of events that make up the scene and let readers judge them for themselves. The first paragraph, from "The Country of the Pointed Firs" by Sarah Orne Jewett, describes a land- and seascape in Maine.

> At last it was the time of late summer, when the house was cool and damp in the morning, and all the light seemed to come through green leaves; but at the first step out of doors the sunshine always laid a warm hand on my shoulder, and the clear, high sky seemed to lift quickly as I looked at it. There was no autumnal mist on the coast, nor any August fog; instead of these, the sea, the sky, all the long shoreline and inland hills, with every bush of bay and every fir-top, gained a deeper color and a sharper clearness. There was something shining in the air, and a kind of lustre on the water and the pasture grass—a northern look that, except at this moment of the year, one must go far to seek. The sunshine of a northern summer was coming to its lovely end.

Notice the orderly and natural way the speaker moves her eyes as she leaves the house, first to the sun and the sky, then to the coast, the sea, then back to the land, with its grass, bushes, and trees. This is a good example of the results that come from a paragraph in which the writer puts things in a proper, simple, natural order. Notice that only in the last sentence does she make a judgment; surely, knowing the process by which she has arrived at her judgment, she has earned the right to call the sunshine *lovely*.

The following paragraph is from *Black Lamb and Grey Falcon*, a book about travel and history by Rebecca West, an Englishwoman who travelled wide and well in Yugoslavia a few years before World War II.

> But there was a view: the garden was built on a terrace high above the domes and minarets and russet roofs of Skoplje, and showed us the green hills surrounding the town, spiked with the white toothpicks of nameless Moslem graves, and the bare blue mountains beyond, shadowed violet by the passing clouds. Our Western conscientiousness made us go to look at this view from the best advantage, and we went to the wall of the garden, where we forgot our purpose, for the hills fell steeply to a street where people of a wild and harlequin sort were leading an entertaining life. A load of hay had been flung up against the wall of one house, and was munched by three ponies, rawboned and flea-bitten. Another house, which had a square of periwinkle blue affixed on its white front for no particular reason, had a mistress who was evidently an indefatigable, but eccentric housewife; through its door there flew every few minutes a jet of water from an emptied basin, discharged with the extreme of shrewishness. Outside another house sat a pretty woman and two pretty girls, smiling and bright-eyed in perpetual pleasure, cooking something on a tiny brazier and drinking from an amphora they passed from one to another. One had a kerchief, one a jacket, one trousers, of bright, rich, shallow red. Soon they noticed that we were watch-

ing them, and cried out to us and waved their long narrow hands, and presently, as if to show off their treasures, one of the girls ran into the house and came out laughing, holding up a baby for our admiration, naked and kicking and lustrous brown.

In this description the development moves quite naturally, as the eye would move, from the general panorama of the town out to the hills and the mountains, and back to the town with its buildings, then to a small group of women, and finally comes to rest on the smallest thing in the scene—a baby held up for inspection and, of course, admiration. It is fitting that the paragraph end with the baby, for in the little universe of this scene the baby has already become the dominant and most active object in it.

How many words of subjective feeling, or judgment, can you find in the paragraph? Maybe half a dozen? Are they absolute judgments or do they simply suggest that this is the way these things seemed or appeared to be?

EXERCISE 58   *Write a paragraph in which you describe a scene in nature, or on a street in town, or a combination of the two, or describe a gathering of people.*

EXERCISE 59   *Write a paragraph describing a person. See as an example the Ramon-Orestes paragraph from* Living Poor, *but in your paragraph describe only one person.*

As this chapter has pointed out, there are six basic methods for developing ideas in a paragraph, according to the particular needs of the paragraph: classification, definition, comparison-contrast, comparison-contrast definition, process, and description. There are, of course, other methods, but we think these six will be the most useful to you in your studies of basic composition.

Be sure, however, not to think that all paragraphs belong exclusively to any one particular class or method. To illustrate our discussions some of our paragraphs have been predominantly of one class. But, in fact, most paragraphs contain elements of at last two or more methods. We believe that what is important for you is the development of the habit of easily, almost automatically, using whatever method or combination of methods suit your purposes. To this end, then, learning the names of these methods and becoming familiar with their uses will be valuable to you because it will help to impress them on your mind and memory.

SUMMARY

1. Basically, most writing is either exposition or narration. Exposition expresses thoughts and ideas; narration tells about something that happened and can be fictional or nonfictional.
2. What you want to say determines which method or methods you use to say it.
3. The six fundamental types dealt with in this chapter are classification, definition, comparison-contrast, comparison-contrast definition, process, and description.
   a. Classification: arranging your material into orderly groups, categories, or classes
   b. Definition: designating (pointing out) and limiting the characteristics and qualities of a thing that distinguish it from all other things, telling what it is
   c. Comparison-contrast: distinguishing two or more things in relation to each other by showing their similarities and differences
   d. Comparison-contrast definition: defining something by comparing and/or contrasting it with something else.
   e. Process: showing the steps in or ways of doing or making something
   f. Description: using words to pictorialize something to make the reader see in the mind's eye the thing as it actually is
4. Although one method usually predominates in a paragraph, other methods often appear in the same paragraph.

EXERCISE 60 *Identify and name the different methods of development used in the paragraph below, from Martin Luther King, Jr.'s "Letter From Birmingham Jail."*

Now what is the difference between the two [just and unjust laws]? How does one determine when a law is just or unjust? A just law is a man-made code that squares with the moral law or the law of God. An unjust law is a code that is out of harmony with the moral law. To put it in the terms of Saint Thomas Aquinas, an unjust law is a human law that is not rooted in eternal and natural law. Any law that uplifts human personality is just. Any law that degrades human personality is unjust. All segregation statutes are unjust because segregation distorts the soul and damages the personality. It gives the segregator a false sense of superiority and the segregated a false sense of inferiority. To use the words of Martin Buber, the great Jewish philosopher, segregation substitutes an "I-it" relationship for the "I-thou" relationship and ends up relegating persons to the status of things. So segregation is not only politically, economically, and sociologically unsound, but is morally wrong and sinful. Paul Tillich has said that sin is separation. Isn't segregation an existential expression of man's tragic separation, and expression of his awful estrangement, his terrible sinfulness? So I can urge men to obey the 1954 decision of the Supreme Court because it is morally right, and I can urge them to disobey segregation ordinances because they are morally wrong.

EXERCISE 61   *Identify and name the methods of development used by Rebecca West in a paragraph from her* Black Lamb and Grey Falcon *that describes King Milutin of Serbia in the fourteenth century.*

He worked marvels for his country, but was untender to many of his subjects. He hungered hotly for women, but was cold as ice when he discarded them or used them as political instruments. He was ardently devout, but used his religion as a counter in his international relationships without showing a sign of scruple. There is robustness in him that charms from the yonder side of the grave, but without doubt his vitals were eaten by the germ of melancholy. His picture is among the frescoes here. He stands, deeply bearded, in the costume worn by Serbian royalty, which is clearly imitated from the Byzantine mode: a stiff tunic of rich material studded with jewels, which disregards the frailty of the enclosed flesh and constrains it to magnificence. That costume powerfully recalls the later Tudor portraits, the gorgeous robes that held together the grossness of Henry VIII and brain-raddled emaciation of Elizabeth and presented them as massive monarchs. Such vestments speak of a world founded on the idea of status, which regarded a king as the beloved deputy of God, not because he was any particular sort of man, but because it was considered obvious that if he were crowned a king he would try to act like a beloved deputy of God, since society had agreed that was how a king should act. There stands beside him, equally sumptuous, his wife Simonis, the daughter of the Byzantine Emperor Andronicus II. She was Milutin's fourth wife. He had had to work up to her, earning the right through a long life to avenge an early disappointment.